STRESS-PROOF
your
LIFE

HIGH PERFORMANCE UNDER PRESSURE

STRESS-PROOF
your
LIFE

ELIZ GREENE

Published and distributed by:
SOUND WISDOM
P.O. Box 310
Shippensburg, PA 17257-0310
717-530-2122

info@soundwisdom.com

www.soundwisdom.com

Cover/jacket designer: Eileen Rockwell

ISBN 13 TP: 978-1-64095-161-7

ISBN 13 eBook: 978-1-64095-162-4

For Worldwide Distribution, Printed in the U.S.A.

1 2 3 4 5 6 7 8 / 25 24 23 22 21

To Clay: You are my rock and my best friend. Thank you for always being on my side.

To Grace and Callie:
For years I've been telling the story of the moments I looked forward to as you grew up. You have become amazing women, and I can't wait to see what you do next.

CONTENTS

Introduction   Are You Too Stressed to
Read a Book on Stress?...................... 9

Section 1   **Treating Stress Management
as a HARD Skill** **15**

Chapter 1   A New Kind of Stress Management 17

Chapter 2   How Stressed Are You?...................... 27

Section 2   **Overcoming Overwhelm** **31**

Chapter 3   The Crisis of Urgency 33

Chapter 4   How Overwhelming Is Your
Stress Environment? 37

Chapter 5   Practicing Stress Ecology.....................51

Section 3   **Combating Uncertainty** **67**

Chapter 6   Uncertainty Is Paralyzing 69

Chapter 7   Manufacturing Security...................... 79

Chapter 8   Practicing Manufactured Security 91

Section 4   **Offsetting the Physical Impact of Stress 99**

Chapter 9   Cortisol Is the Problem 101

Chapter 10   How Much Damage Is Your Stress Causing? . 107

Chapter 11   Practicing Physical Stress Offset 127

Section 5   **Recovering from Psychological Stress 163**

Chapter 12   What Keeps You Up at Night? 165

Chapter 13   What Is Your Stress Recovery Personality? 171

Chapter 14   Practicing Stress Recovery 187

Section 6   **Resilience in Crisis and Change 201**

Chapter 15   Trouble in the Bubble 203

Chapter 16   Practicing Resilience 209

Conclusion   Practicing a Stress-Proof Lifestyle 231

                Executive Summary 241

                Stress-Proof Leadership Insights 257

                About Eliz Greene 289

                Connect with Eliz Greene 293

                Where's Your Proof? 295

                Who's Who in This Book .307

                Gratitude 313

ARE YOU TOO STRESSED TO READ A BOOK ON STRESS?

get it.

We are all busy, and the swirl of demands from work and home, combined with a 24-hour news cycle, causes unrelenting overwhelm, uncertainty, and STRESS. We all need to live and work well under that pressure.

I wrote *Stress-Proof Your Life* as a guide for people who are dealing with unrelenting stress caused by overwhelm and uncertainty. This book treats stress management as a data-driven HARD skill. The assessments, strategies, and tools are designed to help you manage your stress environment and put simple practices into place to protect yourself from unavoidable stress and support your quality of life and performance.

Don't let this book stress you out!

Stress Detour
Don't have time to read the whole book? Skip ahead to page 241 to read the Executive Summary.

The point of this book is to tame stress. If you are overwhelmed by any of the exercises, DON'T STRESS! You have my permission to skip ahead. In fact, there are stress detours like the one above throughout the book to help you navigate to the strategies you need.

To get you started, here are a few ways you can use this book:

- **If you are the kind of person who likes to do all of the quizzes, write in the book, and delve into the data**, read the book cover to cover and enjoy!
- **If your company assigned this book or you really don't have time to read the whole thing**, skip ahead to the Executive Summary starting on page 241. There you'll find a brief description of each of the skills covered in the book. You'll not only be familiar with the content of the book; you'll also be able to quickly determine which strategies may be the best fit for you and go directly to those pages.
- **If you are worried about the toll your stress is taking**, skip to Chapter 2 and take the stress level assessment. You'll be guided on where to go next based on the results of the assessment.

Why is stress-proofing essential to quality of life and success?

Stress robs us of the ability to think clearly and creatively, bogs down productivity, hinders decision-making, chills relationships, and damages our health. In fact, job stress has now overtaken smoking as the primary cause of preventable death in the United States. Sadly, most stress management solutions address the wrong problem.

Managing stress is about more than "getting your ducks in a row." We often believe our disorganization or a lack of inner strength causes stress, but it doesn't.

What is really causing productivity-stealing, life-threatening stress?

Caring for children or elders, arguing with a colleague, or having a leaky roof can be stressful, but chronic high stress—the kind that kills—is caused by overwhelm and uncertainty. How do I know?

For nearly two decades I've traveled the country speaking about wellness and stress. A few years ago, I began conducting an international study to quantify the problem of work-life balance, hoping to provide best-practice solutions to the thousands of people I reach each year. I was shocked by what I learned. I used an online testing instrument to survey nearly 4,000 people across a spectrum of organizations and industries, including UPS, Colgate-Palmolive, NASA, hospital systems, independently owned retail businesses, tech companies, financial services, and institutions of higher education. Almost universally—across all generations and genders—the workers who responded told me they were stressed about things other than work-life balance issues and said that something different than work-life balance, mindfulness, or time management strategies would reduce their stress.

Overwhelm and uncertainty caused by issues outside their individual control were the cause of stress for 90 percent of people. This seemed very familiar to me. I had a near-fatal heart attack at age 35 while 7 months pregnant with twins. Recovering from open-heart surgery and a cesarean section while caring for premature twins was absolutely overwhelming and my health was uncertain. The skills I developed to protect my heart from stress and support the life I want were the beginnings of the stress-proofing process that I share with audiences around the world today.

This book is the culmination of years spent working with high performers, my survival experience, and that research. My work uncovered six problems created by high levels of stress:

1. High stress destroys the capacity for a purposeful and enjoyable life.
2. Overwhelm amps up stress.
3. Uncertainty crowds out rational thought.
4. High stress causes physical damage.
5. Psychological stress keeps cortisol flowing.
6. Vulnerability impedes resilience in crisis and change.

Each of the following sections offers research-based insight on the impact of stress and techniques for building specific skills to become immune to it.

Section 1: Treating Stress Management as a HARD Skill: We deserve better than a throwing-spaghetti-at-the-wall approach to stress. Too often stress management is delivered as an afterthought in wellness. We all know we need to reduce stress, but there is little examination of what is causing the stress, what stressors can be eliminated, and how to deal with stress we can't avoid. Stress-proofing is a data-driven process that will enable you to identify the causes of stress and protect your physical health, emotional well-being, and capacity for creativity and critical thought.

Section 2: Overcoming Overwhelm: Quiet the cry of swirling overwhelm through a series of steps to identify what is causing stress in your environment, and practice stress ecology to reorder your environment to support vitality. This helps you focus on what's most essential and then use that focus to improve your quality of life and performance.

Section 3: Combating Uncertainty: Under stress, our brains depend on instinct rather than rational thought because the part of the brain responsible for critical thinking is busy dealing with the psychological reaction to stress. This reaction not only impedes productivity, but it can also create a paralyzing loop of anxiety. The strategies in this section address how to manufacture security to deal with the stress of uncertainty.

Section 4: Offsetting the Physical Impact of Stress: Stress can rob years from your life by exponentially increasing your risk of heart disease and other conditions. Offsetting this impact is essential to becoming immune to unavoidable stress. This section uses a series of assessments to evaluate the physical impact of your stress and provides a bank of strategies to offset it.

Section 5: Recovering from Psychological Stress: This section explores how to disengage from stressors to allow your body to recover from psychological stress. Discovering your stress recovery personality will enable you to identify which activities best promote your recuperation.

Section 6: Resilience in Crisis and Change: Getting comfortable with vulnerability is the key to being resilient. Life-threatening or life-altering events such as divorce, serious illness, and accidents leave us feeling helpless, unsafe, and weak—vulnerable. When we feel vulnerable, our natural inclination is to pull into ourselves for protection. Vulnerability makes it more challenging to engage in the world around us, connect with people who can help us, and feel good. These chapters offer strategies for getting comfortable with vulnerability so you can implement the stress-proof skills.

Stress-proof leadership insights

Everyone, regardless of their job or industry, will benefit from the stress-proofing strategies detailed in this book. But leaders will find the principles particularly relevant. My audiences are filled with middle managers, small business owners, and executives struggling under the burden of stress, and I've interviewed more than 100 leaders for the book. These leaders carry the weight of their own stress and then lay awake at night because they've seen how stress is tanking their teams' performance. They often sacrifice themselves to insulate their people from pressure and an overwhelming workload. The pressure of being squeezed between expectations from above and keeping a team sane is the most common thread I hear in interviews with stressed-out leaders.

Stress-proof skills are essential for leaders to protect their own health, success, and quality of life. In addition, starting on page 257 I offer insights from my research on what works to reduce stress and support performance in the workplace and what doesn't.

Why this book?

Our high-pressure lives are taking a toll on our health, performance, and quality of life. My hope is that you will use this book to withstand high stress, change, crisis, and to bounce back from illness—because you deserve a fulfilling and enjoyable life.

Are you ready to live and work well under pressure?

SECTION 1

**Treating Stress Management
as a HARD Skill**

Chapter 1

A NEW KIND OF STRESS MANAGEMENT

 The Problem:
High stress destroys the capacity for a purposeful and enjoyable life.

Some stress is natural; too much is a problem.

We can't alleviate all stress, and we wouldn't want to even if we could. Some stress is natural and necessary; it is what gives us the zing of energy to get things done. The zing is the result of the hormone cortisol flooding the system when the body detects danger or stress. Cortisol quickens reactions, increases pulse and blood pressure, and even thickens the blood (to prevent bleeding to death in case of injury).

Trouble comes when that zing becomes a constant thrum, continually triggering the cortisol response rather than allowing it to ebb and flow as we need it. Thicker blood, higher blood pressure, and increased pulse all make the heart work harder, which is why prolonged high stress doubles the risk of heart attack and stroke.

Too much stress destroys health and performance.

High cortisol levels caused by stress eat away at physical health, often in unexpected ways like it did for Miranda:

Miranda came to the doctor, thinking the dogs gave her poison ivy, but she was wrong. She looked down at her bare leg peeking out from the examination gown as she waited for the doctor. She'd been so tired lately, which isn't surprising. As the managing editor for a start-up news website, Miranda was working long hours under intense pressure. She'd also been achy, which probably meant she had caught whatever her assistant's kids were sick with last week. Now, however, there is a weird rash on her leg.

She is only 34—how can she possibly have shingles? Isn't that an older person's disease? The doctor isn't surprised, however. She tells Miranda that the pace at which she's been working is putting too much pressure on her body and has weakened her immune system as a result. There is a vaccine now for shingles.

Too bad there isn't a vaccine to immunize her against stress!

Or is there? The key to developing any vaccine is isolating the cause of the disease. Similarly, building immunity to stress requires identifying the cause. Too often work-life balance is identified as the cause of stress.

However, my research shows that the vast majority of stress is caused by overwhelm, uncertainty, and work culture. It makes sense to focus attention on those issues, but unfortunately, for most of us, changing them is outside of our control. For example, low staff levels cause stress because employees have to take on additional work and worry their evaluation will suffer. No amount of deep breathing will resolve that situation.

Because the issues of overwhelm, uncertainty, and contagious stress are largely outside of our control, we need to shift our focus from preventing stress to becoming immune to it.

Where's Your Proof?
Check out more information about my study on page 295.

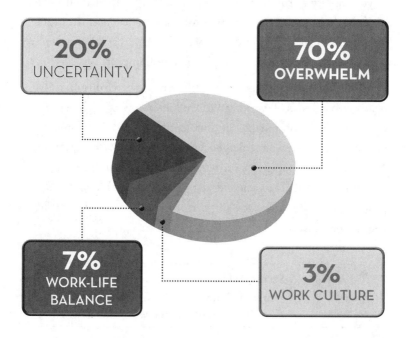

20%
UNCERTAINTY

70%
OVERWHELM

7%
WORK-LIFE
BALANCE

3%
WORK CULTURE

My research has been a backstage pass to see how high-performing, purpose-driven organizations create cultures that are immune to overwhelm and uncertainty. I received volumes of unvarnished truth from the participants in my study. I've seen what works and what doesn't.

Stress management should be treated as a HARD skill essential to quality of life and high performance.

Too many organizations treat stress management as a "nice-to-have" aspect of a wellness program. Dealing with the impact of high levels of stress is essential to protecting your quality of life, your health, as well as your ability to think critically and creatively. Rather than slapping work-life balance strategies or mindfulness practices over the problem, stress-proofing uses data and a set of skills to address the root cause of stress as well as its physical and psychological impact.

The stress-proofing method pulls from my research on job stress and nearly two decades of working with and interviewing high performers operating in environments of unrelenting stress. I developed the system with input from emergency room nurses, construction firms, NASA, large corporations, start-up companies, manufacturing firms, and others—probably, someone facing stressors just like yours. Stress-proofing your life means you can perform and live an enjoyable life in the face of stress that you cannot avoid.

Stress Detour
Worried about your stress level?
Skip ahead to the assessment in Chapter 2.

Stress-proofing combines skills to limit the physical impact of cortisol, promote stress recovery, and deal with the challenges of overwhelm and uncertainty.

Much like a flu shot can prevent or lessen the impact of influenza, becoming stress-proof means building immunity to stressors you cannot avoid. Stress-proofing protects health and performance against stress using five principles:

- Overcome overwhelm
- Combat uncertainty
- Offset the physical impact of stress
- Recover from psychological stress
- Become resilient in crisis and change

What does a Stress-Proof Life feel like?

In November of 2000, I was seven months pregnant with twins. Preterm labor had landed me in the hospital a month earlier, and I spent those weeks quiet and still in a hospital bed, waiting for the time it would be safe to deliver our girls. Then one Sunday morning, life turned upside down. Something went wrong, and my heart stopped. Luckily, excellent nurses and physicians rushed to my side, restarted my heart, and saved my life and the lives of our daughters.

In a matter of a few hours, I survived a heart attack, cesarean delivery of the girls, and open-heart surgery. In the days that followed, however, something amazing happened. My priorities were crystal

clear. A photo taken eight days after the girls were born tells the story best.

My husband, Clay, and I are in the neonatal intensive care unit (NICU). It is the first time both girls were out of the incubators at the same time and we were able to hold them together.

Everything important to me was right there.

Sure, there was a swirl of worries, pain, and quite a bit of uncertainty. However, in that moment, we existed in a bubble of contentment. I was determined to hang on to that feeling.

A few days later, when visiting the NICU, I remarked to my husband about how loud it was in the room. Machines were beeping, babies were crying, and it was all a bit too much. "It's always been this loud," he responded, "you just didn't notice."

It was true. I had been focused on my bubble of contentment and was able to ignore the swirl of distractions around us. As we left the hospital and reentered life, the swirl of things calling for my time, energy, and attention became more intense, and holding on to that bubble was harder. In the years since, I've dedicated myself to focusing on that bubble of contentment and managing my stress.

Having survived a heart attack, I am already at a high risk of having another one. Prolonged high stress is simply something I can't afford. That doesn't mean life decided to go easy on me. Work, illness, family, finances, and so many things we can't control create stress. Finding a way to insulate myself from the effects of that stress has been essential.

Creating your own bubble, a space in which to live and work well in the midst of swirling overwhelm, uncertainty, and unavoidable stress, is the essential metaphor of being stress-proof.

The power of redefining quality of life and success

Sheila always feels the need to win the "I'm so busy" game. Under constant fear of being judged for not working hard enough, she spends her days taking on every project possible. She wears her busyness as a badge of honor, knowing she appears successful. Getting everything done is often overwhelming, but she delights in the praise she receives as a woman who "does it all." Sheila's conversations with friends and co-workers devolve into a competition to prove who is the busiest. She regularly fears people will figure out she is just pretending to have it all together.

In centuries past, the outward sign of success was the ability to have leisure time. Wealthy, successful people had ample food and were able to weigh more. Their hands were soft and their clothing impractical for physical labor. More recently, possessions became the outward sign of success. People demonstrated their wealth and success by the type of homes and cars they purchased, as well as exotic vacations and luxury leisure items such as boats and second homes. In this century, the signs have flipped. Yes, possessions are still an important sign of success, but more often the coveted possessions are technologies that enable us to stay connected and work from anywhere.

> We need to change our focus from the volume of tasks we can endure to the amount of purpose we can create.

Now, a time-demanding career is perceived as the ultimate sign of success. Leisure is no longer valued and is often considered a sign of laziness. Even parents who stay home to raise children feel the pressure to appear busy to be perceived as successful. For example, Alan left a career as an economist to raise his children and now refers to himself as a "professional parent." He sits on every committee for school and church and feels compelled to give of his time even if he doesn't enjoy the work.

Both Sheila and Alan put on an act to convince themselves and others of their accomplishments, but neither feels fulfilled, just busy. When the benchmark of success is the sheer volume of tasks we can endure, how can anyone feel satisfied or successful? How can we have a high quality of life when we are measuring the wrong things?

Alan shouldn't devalue the purpose in raising human beings who will contribute to the world. Sheila needs a new measure of her worth and purpose.

Quality of life is often defined as avoiding bad health outcomes. Sure, we'd all like to avoid the stress that causes an increased risk of cancer or heart disease. No one wants weight gain, muscle weakness, mood swings, depression, or irritability. But to me, we should focus on something more than avoiding bad consequences. Vitality encompasses everything we need to support and enjoy a purposeful life. Good physical health, emotional resilience, and mental acuity are essential to vitality.

Vitality is the capacity for a purpose-driven life—the power to survive and grow.

Stress-Proof Leadership Insight
Leaders typically believe they know what is causing stress in their team and commit time and money to addressing those issues. They are often wrong.
Read about this insight on page 283.

High cortisol levels eat away at physical health and emotional well-being and interfere with critical thought.

Too much stress destroys vitality.

Each of the following sections illustrate:

- How overwhelm creates a crisis of urgency that intensifies stress.
- How uncertainty robs you of critical thought.

- How the stress reaction threatens your health.
- How psychological stress impedes recovery.
- How vulnerability in crisis and change creates stress.

Understanding how stress is generated makes it possible to choose the right skills and strategies to become immune to its impact.

Stress-proofing isn't a destination.

Stress-proofing is a practice that needs to be revisited regularly. The next chapter has an assessment to evaluate your stress level. Retaking that assessment after you've implemented the stress-proof skills for 30, 60, or 90 days is a measurable indication of your progress in reducing and becoming immune to unavoidable stress.

Make a commitment to do the work.

Stress-proofing uses a set of skills to nullify the physical and psychological effects of high stress and support vitality—but it takes effort to implement those skills.

It is time to treat stress management as a HARD SKILL that is essential to a purpose-driven, enjoyable life.

Let's stress-proof your life!

Chapter 2

HOW STRESSED ARE YOU?

Stress-Proof Assessment

The Stress Level Index

C ortisol itself isn't the problem. The physical and psychological reactions in the body to sustained high levels of cortisol cause damage over time. Unlike high cholesterol, there isn't an effective blood test to evaluate cortisol levels. Paying attention to the symptoms of stress is the best way to evaluate the potential for damage. With diverse symptoms such as irritability, stomach upset, and sleeplessness, stress is often challenging to quantify.

I developed the Stress Level Index as part of my research on job stress. The result of this index indicates how likely it is that your stress will impact your physical health, quality of life, and performance.

Think about a typical week. Use the worksheet on page 29 to keep track of how often you experience the things described below. Simply put an "X" in the appropriate space for each statement.

How often (*never, some of the time, about half of the time, most of the time,* or *always*) do you experience the following:

- Feeling overwhelmed by the number of things to be done in the time allowed
- Sleeping less than seven hours at night

- Taking on tasks because others aren't doing them or aren't doing them well enough
- Skipping a meal or grabbing something unhealthy because you are too busy
- Worrying something will "fall through the cracks"
- Feeling unable to prioritize because there is too much to do
- Neglecting important things or people
- Missing out on activities you enjoy
- Having trouble falling asleep because you are thinking about what needs to be done or about an uncertain future
- Dwelling on mistakes or things left undone
- Taking on tasks to protect other people's balance, reputation, or job
- Worrying about making a mistake
- Feeling angry or frustrated about something your boss did (or didn't do)
- Feeling annoyed, distracted, or "dumped on" by a co-worker
- Worrying about your health
- Feeling concerned about money
- Spending time at work thinking about personal issues
- Spending time at home thinking about work issues

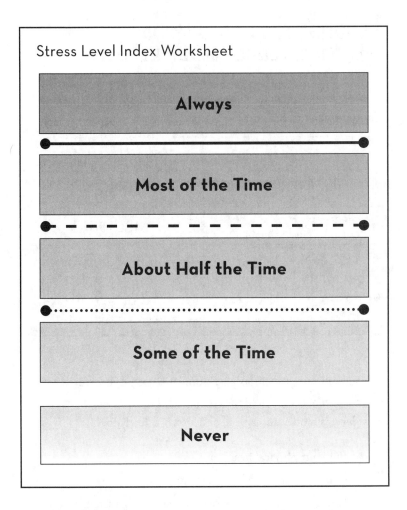

Stress Level Index Worksheet

Always

Most of the Time

About Half the Time

Some of the Time

Never

Stress Detour

If your stress level is critical or acute:

Skip ahead to Sections 4 and 5 to reduce the physical and psychological toll of your stress before exploring how to deal with overwhelm and uncertainty.

🔍 UNDERSTANDING YOUR STRESS LEVEL INDEX RESULTS

Look at where your marks are clustered on the worksheet in relation to the three lines.

Where are your marks?	Stress Level Index
Most marks below the dotted line	**Mild**
Most marks between the dotted line and the dashed line	**Moderate**
Most marks between the dashed line and the solid line	**Critical**
Most marks above the dashed line	**Acute**

Using this assessment as part of my research, I discovered that 70 percent of people evaluated their stress level as critical or acute. If your stress level is moderate, critical, or acute, it is likely to:

- Put your physical health at risk
- Cause psychological stress symptoms
- Decrease your capacity for creativity and critical thought

As I mentioned earlier, stress isn't a bad thing, but prolonged high levels of stress cause physical and emotional harm. Now that you have an idea of your stress level, we can start the process of becoming immune to the effects. The next section of the book discusses how to overcome overwhelm so that you can begin to lessen your stress level and regain your vitality.

SECTION 2

Overcoming Overwhelm

Chapter 3

THE CRISIS OF URGENCY

The Problem:
Overwhelm
intensifies stress.

Overwhelm creates a crisis of urgency.

I n our busy lives, we rarely stop to examine the swirl of demands for our time, energy, and attention. Overwhelm makes us feel like we can't keep up. Many of us resonate with Han's experience:

Sticky notes frame Han's office computer screen with reminders of things he is afraid to forget. More notes are stuck to his dashboard and on his home computer. Changes in the economy have been good for his company, and his workload has increased significantly, leaving him struggling to manage the uptick in production. He has always performed well at work, but now he lives in fear of letting something slip. It is the same story at home. Last month he completely forgot to pay the water bill. Sure, it comes only once a quarter, but he is usually on top of things. There is too much to do, too little time, and everything is screaming at him at the same volume.

All of Han's sticky notes, as well as the demands on his time, energy, and attention, create a crisis of urgency. If everything is urgently important, nothing can be a priority. What often is blamed on a lack of organization or poor time management usually turns out to be an overwhelm-induced confusion of urgency.

We live in an environment of stress.

Stress-Proof Leadership Insight
Other stressors impact reactions to overwhelm.
Read about this insight on page 277.

An environment is the collection of things, people, conditions, and forces that surround us. A stress environment is made up of the swirl of things, activities, obligations, people, conditions, and forces calling for your time, energy, and attention.

Stress-proofing stifles the cry of things, people, and obligations calling for our time, energy, and attention; promotes satisfaction and productivity; and insulates us from unrelenting stress.

The first step of taming overwhelm is getting a clear look at the items in your personal stress environment and how much they add to or detract from your vitality. This chapter puts sticky notes to better use by walking through how to diagram your personal stress environment and evaluate the items in it.

Over the years, audience members and participants in training programs have loved and profoundly benefited from these activities. Facilitating this process and the discussion that follows has allowed me to witness vivid moments of clarity as people recognize the real cost of overwhelm.

This process started with my own sticky note moment of clarity. As a solo practitioner of an odd profession, it is easy for me to get overwhelmed by my own swirl of obligations. Several years ago, three other professional speakers and I created a mastermind group. While none of us live in the same state, we act as each other's co-workers and often as a quasi-board of directors for each business. We talk regularly on online video calls and get together in person each year to work on our businesses.

At first, still invested in appearing to have everything together, I was fairly guarded. I didn't want them to judge me for the chaos in my world. I asked for some feedback but didn't reveal too much. However, once we built trust, and perhaps spurred on by a bottle of wine, I decided to let them see what was stopping my success. As a person with an office supply buying issue, I always have a few packs of sticky notes in my bag. The night before it was my time to be in the "hot seat," I wrote out all of the things calling for my time, energy, and attention, each on its own note.

In the morning, I laid it all out on the table, literally. As I described each issue and covered the table with sticky notes, I became more and more anxious. In the end, I looked down and declared, "This is why I can't get anything done."

The volume of notes was overwhelming for all of us, but my friends started to pick up one note at a time and ask questions about it.

- "Is this important?"
- "Do you like doing this?"
- "Does this make you money?"

When we came to one project, which I declared to be a splendid idea, I had to admit it was:

Earning me no money.

Costing me significant money to develop.

Draining my energy, because I wasn't excited about the work.

My colleague Thom crumpled up the sticky note and threw it on the floor. Seeing it on the floor took my breath away! He just threw away something calling for my time, energy, and attention. It was scary, but also freeing. It also reminded me of something I've taught for years:

> Saying "no" to something means emphatically saying "yes" to what is important.

I was reminded that if I took more notes off the table, I would have more time for what matters most. If I sorted the swirl of things calling for my time, energy, and attention, I would have more capacity to be purposeful in my work and focus more on my quality of life. As we sorted through the sticky notes, my group helped me eliminate some activities, reevaluate others, and elevate what was most important. I was left with a finite group of people, activities, and projects. In the following six months, I was more successful and content in my work and my personal life than I had been in years. By identifying and taming my stress environment, I increased my vitality, as well as my capacity for a purpose-driven and enjoyable life.

The next chapter has an exercise to help you sort your stress environment. This exercise is the centerpiece of the workshops I facilitate for highly stressed executives, managers, and business owners.

Chapter 4

HOW OVERWHELMING IS YOUR STRESS ENVIRONMENT?

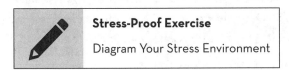

Stress-Proof Exercise

Diagram Your Stress Environment

There are five steps to diagramming your stress environment.

1. Identify the items calling for your time, energy, and attention.
2. Determine the organization of your stress environment.
3. Evaluate the expenditure on and benefits of the items.
4. Examine the impact of your stress environment on your capacity for a purpose-driven life.
5. Sort the items by their value.

Step 1: Identify the items calling for your time, energy, and attention.

Supplies:

- 50–100 sticky notes (2" x 2" or 3" x 3" work well)

- A large space on a table, desk, or floor
- A pen
- Your phone (to take pictures)

Use the following prompts to catalog the items in your stress environment. Write a single item on each sticky note. These items may be work-related or personal. These may be things you enjoy or things you dislike. Don't worry about judging these activities; simply record what is calling for your time, energy, and attention.

Think about the past three months.

- What household duties do you spend time completing (e.g., cooking, shopping, cleaning, yard work, etc.)?
- What routine work tasks do you complete each day (e.g., e-mail, expense recording, filling out time sheets, etc.)?
- What personal tasks do you complete each day?
- What projects, at work or at home, are in progress?
- What work relationships regularly take your time, energy, and attention?
- If you have children, what parenting duties require your time (e.g., transportation, homework help, hygiene, etc.)?
- What relationship-building activities, at work or personally, do you do (e.g., date night, work outings, networking groups, clubs, etc.)?
- What hobbies do you enjoy?
- Do you play recreational sports?
- What social obligations or commitments do you have (e.g., family events, alumni groups, etc.)?
- What volunteer or service roles do you have?

- What professional development or continuing education activities do you do?
- Do you care for or make time to visit extended family members?

Stress Detour
Do you really need to write all of these sticky notes?

Maybe. Part of what makes this process valuable is having a visual representation of your stress environment. There is power in seeing the sheer number of things calling for your time, energy, and attention.

Moving the sticky notes around is a kinesthetic learning activity that solidifies the evaluation of these items.

BUT—if this is stressing you out, skip ahead to the strategies in the next chapter.

- What significant life changes are in process or coming up (e.g., wedding, moving, graduation, death of a loved one, retirement, baby, adoption, divorce, financial setback, traumatic event, etc.)?
- Are you dealing with a health issue, personally or in your immediate family?
- What did you used to enjoy doing but don't have time to do anymore?
- What keeps you up at night? (What are you worrying about, such as layoffs, the national economy, relationship issues, uncertainty, etc.?)

- What do you do to care for yourself, physically and emotionally?
- What do you do to feed your mind, beyond professional development?
- Are you active in a community of faith?
- What should you be doing, at work or personally, but never seem to have the time to complete?
- What do you want to be doing but rarely can fit in the time to do it?
- Are you active in political or social justice efforts?

At the end of Step 1, you should have a collection of sticky notes that represent the items in your stress environment. The more specific you are in this process, the more effective the following steps will be in sorting your environment.

 Take a moment to reflect on the sticky notes you've created.

- Do they accurately represent how you spend your time, energy, and attention?
- Do you need to add anything?
- How do you feel about the number of notes you've created?

Step 2: Determine the organization of your stress environment.

Think about how much time, energy, and attention you devote to the items on each sticky note. Indicate the expenditure you make for each item:

- Significant expenditure of time, energy, and attention: write an "S" on the note.
- Modest expenditure of time, energy, and attention: write an "M" on the note.
- Negligible expenditure of time, energy, and attention: write an "N" on the note.

Use the Stress Environment Model below to organize your sticky notes. You can draw the model on a large piece of paper or simply place the notes as indicated below. A large, printable version is available for download at StressProof.Life.

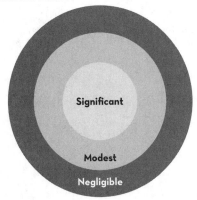

- Place notes marked with an "S" in the center.
- Place notes marked with an "M" in the middle ring.
- Place notes marked with an "N" in the outer ring.

Take a moment to reflect on where your sticky notes are placed. The notes in the center of the model take most of your time, energy, and attention. The notes on the outside of the model get very little time, energy, and attention.

- Does it accurately represent how you spend your time, energy, and attention?
- Do you need to move anything?
- How do you feel about the notes you marked with an "S"?

_____

_____

_____

_____

- How do you feel about the notes you marked with an "N"?

_____

_____

_____

_____

Step 3: Evaluate the expenditure on and benefits of the items.

Each item on your sticky notes can support or inhibit your vitality. The Vitality Quotient (VQ) measures the value of an item to your capacity and quality of life compared to the amount of time, energy, or attention it requires. When our brains determine that the time, energy, and emotion an activity costs us is higher than the tangible and intangible benefits it brings, our stress reaction triggers. We all are constantly—usually subconsciously—running a simple, quantifiable analysis of the ways we spend our time, asking ourselves, "Is this worth it?"

Stress Detour
Have you written 100 sticky notes and now wonder whether you really need to figure out a VQ for each of them?
Pick 20 or so sticky notes, figure out the VQ for those items, and then move on. You can always come back and do more.

A. For each item, how do you feel when doing this activity, interacting with the person, or working on the project?

- exhilarated
- gratified
- useful
- indifferent
- bored
- disheartened
- pessimistic
- wounded

B. Evaluate each item using the Vitality Quotient Table:

Locate the expenditure and benefit you indicated for each item in the table. Write the quotient on the sticky note.

Understanding the Vitality Quotient

Vitality Quotient Table			
	Significant Expenditure	Modest Expenditure	Negligible Expenditure
Benefit			
Exhilarated	1	1.5	2.7
Gratified	0.8	1.2	2.3
Useful	0.7	1	2
Indifferent	0.6	0.8	1.6
Bored	0.4	0.7	1.3
Disheartened	0.3	0.5	1
Pessimistic	0.2	0.3	0.7
Wounded	0.1	0.2	0.3

Stress-Proof Leadership Insight

Effective leaders solve problems so their people can work at their highest potential.

Read about this insight on page 261.

When we feel like we are getting a bad deal, psychological stress is triggered. Inequity between the expenditure and the benefit creates stress. The Vitality Quotient indicates the equity between the time, energy, and attention you expend and the benefit you receive. As illustrated by the Vitality Quotient Scale below:

- If the VQ is 1, the activity is neutral. It provides an equivalent amount of benefit for the expenditure.

- If the VQ is less than 1, the activity is draining. The benefit is not enough to compensate for the expenditure, and it detracts from your capacity for a purposeful life.

- If the VQ is more than 1, the activity enhances your capacity. The higher the VQ, the more your vitality is supported and nurtured.

Detracts	Equivalent	Enhances
0.1	1	2.7

Vitality Quotient

Step 4: Examine your stress environment.

Use your phone to take a picture of your sticky notes placed in the Stress Environment Model for use in the next chapter. Ideally, high-Vitality Quotient items would be closest to the center. For most of us, however, that may not be the case.

In Chapter 7, we will continue to tame overwhelm by reordering your personal stress environment, but first, take a moment to reflect on the VQ of the notes closest to the center of your stress environment. The notes in the center of the model take most of your time, energy, and attention, whereas the notes on the outside of the model get very little time, energy, and attention.

- Does the arrangement accurately reflect how you feel about these items?
- Do you need to move anything?
- How do you feel about the VQs of the items closest to the middle of your model? Are there low-VQ items taking significant time, energy, and attention?

- Are there high-VQ items toward the outside of your model? Which activities would you like to invest more time, energy, and attention into?

_____

_____

_____

_____

_____

_____

- How overwhelming does your stress environment feel?

_____

_____

_____

_____

_____

_____

Step 5: Sort items by Vitality Quotient.

Now that you've taken a picture of your current stress environment, let's examine the items by their value. Sort the items in your stress environment into three columns, as illustrated in the graphic below.

- Move any sticky note with a VQ of less than 1 into the left ("detracts") column. Place the highest-VQ items at the top of the column.

- Move any sticky note with a VQ of 1 to 1.3 into the center ("equivalent") column. Place the highest-VQ items at the top of the column.

- Move any sticky note with a VQ of 1.5 or more into the right ("enhances") column. Place the highest-VQ items at the top of the column.

	Detracts		Equivalent		Enhances
0.8		1.3		2.7	
0.7		1.2		2.3	
0.6		1		2	
0.5				1.6	
0.4				1.5	
0.3					
0.2					
0.1					

Take a picture of how your sticky notes are ordered now.

Looking at the columns, what do you notice?

- How do you feel about the number of sticky notes in the "detracts" column?

_____

_____

_____

_____

- What insights did you uncover when you placed the sticky notes in the "detracts" column?

_____

_____

_____

_____

- How do you feel about the number of sticky notes in the "enhances" column?

_____

_____

_____

_____

_____

_____

- What insights did you uncover when you placed the sticky notes in the "enhances" column?

_____

_____

_____

_____

_____

_____

Chapter 5

PRACTICING STRESS ECOLOGY

Stress-Proof Skill

Overcome overwhelm by intentionally reordering your stress environment to support vitality.

Taming the swirl of overwhelm

Life and work swirl together. Examining how items interact with each other in your stress environment is important when dealing with overwhelm.

At first, Stephanie was thrilled. Opening a new satellite office in Denver was a great opportunity for her career. Her husband was on board with the idea of moving and immediately began to look at job possibilities. Now, months after uprooting her family, she wonders if it was a good idea after all.

Sure the raise was nice, and a new town is exciting, but now she's the primary breadwinner in the family. This new dynamic in her marriage is chafing a bit. She misses the support of her home office colleagues and her friends in the community. She worries about what this move will cost emotionally in the long run. There are still boxes to unpack, and life seems out of control and overwhelming.

As part of a leadership training, Stephanie defined her stress environment and is overwhelmed at the number of things calling for her time, energy, and attention. She also realizes that vitality-enhancing activities such as time with her husband, taking care of herself, and developing new colleague relationships have been crowded out by putting out fires in her new position. It is time to make some changes.

Ecology is the process of examining and tending to the relationships and interaction of things in your environment. Stress ecology is the process of intentionally reordering the expenditure of time, energy, and attention on the items swirling around us.

Overwhelm is tamed by intentionally reordering your stress environment to support your vitality. The Stress-Proof Ecology Model is a way of understanding how to create the space to live and work well and allow unavoidable stress to swirl outside of it. As a result, you create immunity from the physical and emotional impact of that stress.

Practicing stress ecology is more than moving sticky notes around. It requires examining and evaluating the relationship between the items in your stress environment. When we have our heads down, working hard to try to keep up with demands and obligations, it is often easy to lose sight of the real value of activities and instead focus on the difficulty.

The next phase in the stress-proofing process entails reordering the items in your stress environment by rethinking their value to your capacity for purposeful living. Accordingly, this section walks you through how to place your sticky notes in the Stress-Proof Ecology

Model below. (A large, printable version is available for download at StressProof.Life.)

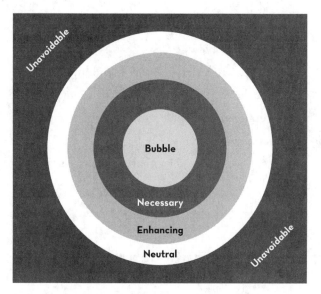

Stress-Proof Ecology Model Layers

- **Bubble:** This layer contains you and the people most important to you. Too often, we fail to place ourselves in the center of our own environment.
- **Necessary:** This layer contains items essential to the survival of the people in the bubble.
- **Enhancing:** This layer contains items bringing contentment and satisfaction.
- **Neutral:** This layer contains items that are neither enhancing nor draining.
- **Unavoidable:** This outer area contains items that have a very low Vitality Quotient but must be kept.

Strategies to overcome overwhelm include:

1. Eliminate detracting items.
2. Identify your bubble.
3. Identify items necessary to support your bubble.
4. Examine the ecology of your stress environment.
5. Pay attention to intangible and ancillary benefits.
6. Elevate enhancing items.
7. Focus on the inside and let unavoidable stress swirl on the outside.

Strategy #1: Eliminate detracting items.

In any environment, there are things to be avoided.

Toxins threaten the health of the system. In a stress environment, toxins are typically projects, perceived obligations, or people who drain our energy and time without providing value in return. Practicing stress ecology requires protecting the system by eliminating items in the "detracts" column and making more time, energy, and attention available to focus on enhancing items.

 Looking at the items in your "detracts" column, are there any you can easily remove? It is okay if nothing immediately jumps out. Think about the following ideas as you contemplate what you can remove from your stress environment.

The discomfort of "no"

We are often uncomfortable letting go, saying "no" to a commitment or obligation. As I mentioned earlier, saying "no" to something means emphatically saying "yes" to what is important. While evaluating the items in the "detracts" column, take a look at the items in the "enhances" column. What enhancing items would you like to invest more time, energy, and attention into? How much more capacity would you create by making that investment? What can you say "no" to in order to make more space for that increased capacity?

If there is a sticky note you can eliminate, crumple it up and throw it away.

The enchanting vacuum of leadership

High-performing people are drawn to leadership roles. This trait is admirable but can create tunnel vision in some situations. In an absence of other leaders, high performers will step in and then persist in the role. This vacuum of leadership is often so enchanting we can't help ourselves. Yet, do we really need to be in charge? Ask yourself some questions about the activity or role:

- Do you really need to do it all yourself?
- Are you the only person able to take the lead?
- Does the position of leadership serve you or your capacity in any way?
- What would happen if you declined the role?

- What else could you do with the time, energy, and attention you invest into this role?

If there is a sticky note you can eliminate, crumple it up and throw it away.

Some toxins are unavoidable.

"I'll take one of these things off the table when I win the lottery!" said a participant at an employee training event for university staff. It's true; sometimes we aren't able to remove items draining the system. The next chapters deal with how to become immune to unavoidable stress. But first, let's continue reordering your stress environment.

Strategy #2: Identify your bubble.

Who needs to be well and secure for you to be content?

Stress Detour
Do you have low-VQ items in your bubble?
Skip ahead to Section 6 to learn about weathering "trouble in the bubble."

Like the bubble of contentment I found in the NICU holding our daughters for the first time, your bubble surrounds you and the people most important to you. Think about laying your head on the pillow at night. Whom do you need to be safe in order to close your eyes and go to sleep? Write each name, including your own, on a separate sticky note (if you don't already have one) and place them in the center of the Stress-Proof Ecology Model.

It is okay to be a little mercenary in this process. A middle-aged audience member at an association event asked, "Do I have to put my mother in my bubble?" My answer was, "Not necessarily. If Mom is part of every day and you play a significant role in keeping her safe and well, then yes, she may belong in your bubble. If Mom is independent, then even though you love her dearly and she's important to you, she is not in your bubble."

Are you alone in your bubble? That is absolutely okay too. We all have different priorities, obligations, and expectations. The bubble represents what needs to be supported by our activities and protected from unavoidable stress.

Strategy #3: Identify items necessary to support the bubble.

The items in this level of the model are essential to the health and success of those people in your bubble. Use the following prompts to move your sticky notes into this level:

- Which items financially support the people in your bubble?

- Which items support your physical and psychological health*? Look in your columns for items having to do with:

❭ Exercise

❭ Eating well

❭ Sleeping

❭ Recovering from psychological stress

- Which items support the physical and psychological health of the other people in your bubble?
- Which items give you a sense of purpose?

Don't worry if you don't have these types of items. Sections 3 and 4 are devoted to creating ways to protect your physical and psychological health.

Take a look at the items in the "necessary" layer. Do they accurately represent the activities, obligations, and demands on your time, energy, and attention that contribute to the well-being and success of the people in your bubble? Do you need to add anything? (If so, be sure to calculate the VQ for that item.)

Strategy #4: Examine the ecology of your stress environment.

Take a look at the items you have not yet placed in the model. Use the following prompts to move them into the appropriate layers:

- Revisit Step 2. Are there any items that no longer seem important? Can you eliminate any of them?
- Place any items left in your "enhances" column in the "enhancing" layer.
- Place any items left in your "equivalent" column in the "neutral" layer.

- Place any items left in your "detracts" column on the outside of the model in the "unavoidable" area.

Take a picture of where your sticky notes are now located. The closer an item is to the bubble, the more time, energy, and attention it should receive. Items necessary to support the bubble are the most important.

Go back and compare this picture with the picture of your original stress environment.

How does your original stress environment differ from the one you created with the Stress-Proof Ecology Model?

_____

_____

_____

_____

When you look at the items in the "necessary" layer, are there more low-VQ items or high-VQ items?

_____

_____

_____

_____

When you think about the items in your "necessary" layer and the value they represent, do they make you more stressed or give you a sense of comfort? How do you think this impacts your life?

_____

_____

_____

_____

The next strategies help you to continue to reorder your stress environment by adjusting the value or importance of your activities.

Strategy #5: Pay attention to intangible and ancillary benefits.

The perceived value of an activity frames how we experience it.

"My job has a VQ of 0.2, but I can't leave it. I need to support my family," said Elijah, a senior manager for a large manufacturing company. As part of the leadership training exercise, he'd placed his job in the "necessary" level. While changes in the economy have been good for his company, work was nonstop, and timelines for project completion were getting shorter and shorter. His expenditure of time, energy, and attention is significant. His salary is in line with *what other people make in similar positions, but it just doesn't feel like enough for the sacrifice he is making.*

As Elijah discussed his job, it became clear that the costs were at the top of his mind, but he had lost sight of many of its benefits. His job provided more than just numbers on a paycheck—it paid for everything his family needed and the majority of what they wanted. These ancillary benefits were valuable. Yes, he determined, the job was one of the most important things, but it also had many intangible benefits, such as the very real value in the relationships with his co-workers. This shift in thinking was pivotal in reevaluating the VQ calculation of his work and reducing stress. How we feel about activities, obligations, and people makes a difference.

Elijah was able to raise the VQ of his job by recognizing that it had both:

Intangible benefits:

- He really enjoys his relationship with his fellow managers and working on the management team.
- He values the mentorship he receives from his boss.
- His team works hard and doesn't drive him nuts (most of the time).
- He is good at his job, and he is proud of the way his team drives a project to completion.
- He is known as a problem solver, and he feels good when others ask for his guidance.

And ancillary benefits:

- The home he can provide for his family is in a nice community, and his kids go to a great school.

- He has enough income to save for his kids' college and for retirement.
- He is encouraged to take his vacation time.
- He loves classic cars, and he just bought a "new" one to restore.

Stress-Proof Leadership Insight
Well-intentioned policies can undermine the value of work.
Read about this insight on page 267.

As Elijah considered the intangible and ancillary benefits, his job didn't swing up to a high VQ in the process, but by reevaluating how he feels about work he was able to raise it to a 0.7, which is much closer to a neutral impact. He also recognized that he needed to start taking some of his accumulated vacation days to reduce his expenditure of time at work. Eventually, he adjusted the VQ of work to 1 and considered it neutral. Moving forward, Elijah committed to reminding himself of the intangible benefits of his job when stress starts building up.

Examine the intangible benefits of the items in your stress environment.

Are there items in your "necessary" layer with low VQs? What intangible benefits do you receive from those items?

What ancillary benefits do you receive from those items?

Are you able to adjust the VQs?

The idea of this strategy is to adjust the VQ of items (if possible) to bring necessary items with low VQs more toward a neutral impact.

Strategy #6: Elevate enhancing items.

Investing in enhancing items softens the impact of detracting items.

Devoting time, energy, and attention to items that enhance your quality of life feels better and increases your capacity to endure items that provide less benefit. Fortunately, this isn't a zero-sum equation. Often a short period of time or a small amount of energy or attention devoted to an enhancing activity is enough to provide significant benefit. All of the items in your stress environment interact with each other.

What activity enhances your quality of life? For some it is a quick run or coffee with a good friend. For others it is hanging out with their dog or cat. Some people enjoy a round of golf; others, sitting down with a good book. So often we feel guilty for spending time on these types of activities, but they are essential to withstanding the cost of stressors outside of your control.

Which items in the "enhancing" layer really should be in the "necessary" layer?

How would it look in your daily or weekly life if you prioritized time to spend on the items you moved?

Strategy #7: Focus on the inside and let unavoidable stress swirl on the outside.

Most of what causes unrelenting stress is outside our control.

We can't control the economy, when people get ill, how the company is run (sometimes even if we own the company), or the weather, but we can create a barrier to protect ourselves from unavoidable stress. Sometimes the things necessary to support the people in our bubble are inherently stressful. Often there are items in the stress environment we can't remove.

Protective gear is essential in many work environments. Wouldn't it be nice to have protective equipment for stress? One of my most popular keynotes, "Donning an Emotional Hazmat Suit," explores this and illustrates a central element of stress ecology. This metaphorical hazmat suit allows someone to work and live safely in the face of unavoidable stress.

The idea of an emotional hazmat suit came to me as I sanded the bottom of our sailboat a few springs ago. Marine bottom paint is toxic. To work safely, I wear a full Tyvek suit, a respirator, gloves, and goggles—essentially a hazmat suit. As I lay beneath the boat, safe in my barrier from the toxic dust falling on me, I had a realization: I needed to create a barrier for the toxic stress falling on me as a school board member.

I thought being on the school board would be just another volunteer position at school. I ran unopposed, and the first few months were enjoyable. I liked my fellow school board members and the administrators. Then a state law gutted teachers unions and fundamentally changed how we dealt with our employees. We needed to create an entirely new set of employee policies and change our compensation system. The teachers were angry, and the community was concerned to the point of panic.

Our formerly sleepy board meetings were suddenly overflowing, and let's just say it is never a good sign when television news cameras show up at your meeting. My phone rang constantly with complaints and questions. We live just a few doors down from the school where our meetings took place, and people would stop me on the way to walk our daughters home to ask questions and make comments. I would walk into meetings and school events with a massive knot in my stomach, knowing I would have to sit silently as people hurled insults at me, my fellow board members, and the administration. It was inescapable.

With a repaired heart, I know that level of stress isn't safe. I couldn't change the anger other people felt. I could only do my best to make the most responsible decisions for the people in our district. I had to find a way to keep all the negativity and stress from impacting my heart.

As I walked into those meetings, I would say to myself,

> **I will not allow things I cannot control to impact my health or my quality of life.**

Reordering the items calling for your time, energy, and attention into an Ecology Model creates a different focus. By concentrating on necessary and enhancing items and limiting the expenditure on items with low VQs that are not necessary for supporting your bubble, you can tame overwhelm. Let the demands of items in the "unavoidable" and "neutral" layers swirl on the outside of your own bubble of contentment.

Sometimes, however, the things necessary to support the people in your bubble are inherently stressful. To that end, Section 4 addresses how to offset the physical impact of unavoidable stress, Section 5 has steps to recover from psychological stress, and Section 6 deals with what to do when there is trouble in the bubble. Feel free to jump ahead to one of those sections now, or continue on to the next section to discover how to combat uncertainty as you build your immunity to stress.

SECTION 3

Combating Uncertainty

Chapter 6

UNCERTAINTY IS PARALYZING

 The Problem:
Uncertainty crowds
out rational thought.

Uncertainty breeds stress and crowds out the ability to think critically and creatively. By understanding how your brain interprets uncertainty and working to manufacture a sense of security, you can reduce stress and support critical thinking and creativity.

Stress caused by uncertainty can be paralyzing.

I forgot that.

Writing a book on stress during our twin daughters' final year of high school was a great way to put my stress-proof strategies to work. But trying to finish the book while preparing to send our twin daughters off for their first year of college proved to be almost impossible.

Our summer was full of dealing with and preparing for uncertainty. Will they be assigned to a good dorm? Will they get a good roommate?

What do they need to pack? How will they get medications? How does food service work?

I made numerous choices that prioritized getting them ready for college over work and writing this book. My days were filled with checklists and shopping. I tried to pack in as much advice as my daughters would tolerate—and shut up when they had had enough. Most of June and July were spent on "last-time" summer experiences and getting them ready for the two different colleges they are attending. August went by far too quickly, and before we knew it, we were moving Grace into her dorm room. Just over two weeks later, we moved Callie into hers.

As we walked away from Callie, leaving her on the steps of the university's iconic chapel, I realized all of the items were checked off. My job preparing them was done. The tears just came. I was unprepared to be as sad as I was returning home without the girls. Clay was sad too. We were sad together. But more than sad, we had an overwhelming sense of uncertainty. We no longer had a direct line to the girls' lives. We were used to daily updates at dinner, checking the online school portal, and being intimately involved in their schedules.

It's not like we didn't know this was coming and weren't excited to see them jump into this new adventure. We planned for this day. Clay and I talked about adjusting our routines at home. I worked for two years to build up my business to keep me busy...and of course, there was writing this book. But even though we communicate with Grace and Callie regularly, we still are left to wonder if they are eating enough, getting enough sleep, going to class, or making friends. It sucks.

I had work to do, but I couldn't get going. I sat in front of the computer and wondered if I'd ever be able to put words together.

What was wrong with me?

In between interviews for the *Food Bullying Podcast* she asked me to co-host, my friend Michele Payn pinpointed the problem: I was having trouble writing about uncertainty because things felt too uncertain.

Who's Who in the Book?
Check out more information about Michele Payn on page 307.

Oh, the irony! Sometimes I need to be reminded of my own material. Here's what I rediscovered about stress caused by uncertainty: you can't be creative or think critically if you are worrying about things you can't control!

Our brains like a predictable environment.

Uncertainty is perceived as unsafe and potentially painful. Whether the situation is predictably positive or predictably negative, your brain prefers something familiar to something unfamiliar. One study determined that people were less stressed by knowing they would receive a small electrical shock than they were by knowing they had an unpredictable chance of being shocked.

Where's Your Proof?
Check out more information about this study on page 302.

Most of us have a relatively small chance of being electrically shocked, but we certainly can encounter shocking situations. For example, if at 4:30 p.m. on a Friday you are called unexpectedly into your boss's office, one of three outcomes is likely:

- You've been doing a great job, things are great, and there is no way you are getting fired.
- You know you are getting fired.
- You are not sure if you are getting fired.

The first and second outcomes are less stressful than the third. The first is predictably positive, so it's not stressful. The second is predictably negative and you can prepare yourself, much like you might grit your teeth if you knew you were about to receive an electrical shock. The third, however, is unpredictable. Unpredictability fires up your brain to get prepared for anything. Your system releases cortisol and other chemicals, which can leave you feeling on high alert.

Once the meeting with your boss is over, your brain calms down. However, what happens if the uncertainty isn't momentary?

Chronic stress caused by uncertainty blocks critical thought.

Our hardwired reaction to feeling unsafe is to protect ourselves and avoid pain. One of the most disastrous effects of chronic high stress is that it blocks critical and creative thought. In other words, the part of the brain responsible for critical thinking is busy dealing with the perceived risk of an unpredictable situation. Our brains don't multitask; they focus on only one thing at a time and then have to switch to the next task. This task-switching not only impedes productivity, but it also creates a paralyzing loop of anxiety when the uncertainty isn't momentary but rather a constant state. The electric shock study also concluded that "people who report higher levels of life stress behave as if they believe that the environment is more uncertain, indicating that chronic stress levels may be affected by prior exposure to environments of high uncertainty."

Stress-Proof Leadership Insight
There are generational differences in how people react to uncertainty.
Read about this insight on page 274.

If we work and think best when we feel secure, how do we counteract the stress caused by long periods of uncertainty?

One of the reasons why news of school shootings, natural disasters, or political discord increases stress is that the information our brains are processing limits our feeling of security. We convince ourselves on a daily basis that potentially dangerous activities are safe so that we can go about our day. If we really thought about the risks of driving on the highway or even crossing a busy street, we would stay in bed and pull the covers over our heads.

You can't just grit your teeth through unrelenting uncertainty. This kind of stress inhibits our ability to succeed and requires a sophisticated set of strategies to move forward with confidence. Remember, our brains like a predictable environment.

We can train our brains to see uncertainty as predictable.

Training allows you to respond to a crisis with confidence. When you know what to do, you can respond intentionally rather than react instinctually. "During a crisis, your brain wants to react instinctually, and often that instinctive response may not be helpful and can even be potentially harmful," explains organizational safety culture expert Lisa Haen. Emergency action professionals such as firefighters, utility workers, and paramedics have to train to be able to work in uncertain, unpredictable situations. Training is essential to reduce risk. "Preparedness in the face of crisis is the key differentiator between body recovery and rescue." In other words, taking proactive measures to prepare for the worst-case scenario makes the situation less likely to result in a catastrophe. Lisa's work with construction, electric utility, and municipal organizations demonstrates that reacting strategically in an emergency situation is a learned behavior that protects us from our natural instinct to react rather than safely respond in an emergency.

Who's Who in the Book?
Check out more information about Lisa Haen on page 308.

This type of training cannot prevent a crisis, but it can control the outcome. Lisa describes the steps of preparedness as follows:

- Identify the potential hazard.
- Determine the proper control measures.
- Create a preparedness plan for crisis.

- Train to develop a safe behavior through awareness of consequence.
- Practice to hardwire muscle memory response.

One of the stories Lisa tells to drive home the importance of training is about a family-run sewer company. Two of the sons of the family and two other employees were working on a job, and the first son went into a manhole; and when he reached the bottom, he fell to the ground and was unconscious. "Going into a manhole may not seem dangerous," explains Lisa. "You open it up and look down and you can't see anything harmful, but oftentimes bad air will sit at the bottom, making it hazardous." The second son went down to save his brother and collapsed at the bottom. The third guy, a friend of the family, looked down the hole, saw the two guys, and jumped down in there. He also succumbed. The fourth guy on the crew was a newer worker. He looked down, saw a problem, and called for help rather than going into the hole. Two would-be rescuers became the victims.

"It really makes my heart hurt when I think about all the fatalities. Simple things could have prevented it. If they just would have tested the air, they would have seen that it wasn't a good environment to go into. But they didn't test the air. If they'd set up a lifeline, when the brother hit that non-oxygen environment they could have pulled him up to safety." she says.

When we prepare for the risks we can predict, we also prepare to respond with confidence when something, like a heart attack or diabetic reaction, happens at the bottom of the manhole. It's all a matter of identifying the hazard, mitigating the hazard, and then training to build that hardwired response so that they're not reacting out of instinct. Engaging in these steps, high-risk workers are able to better prevent a potentially catastrophic event."

We can't always prevent a crisis, but training creates a safer work environment and allows workers to function with a degree of proactive confidence in a dangerous environment. This training and preparation enable the brain to treat an emergency event as predictable and respond in a more rational way. Another way to think about this process is exposure therapy. Let's say you are terrified of snakes. You can train your brain to react more rationally by looking at pictures of snakes and slowly building up your exposure until you can touch a real snake.

The good news is that we can use a similar process to prepare our brains to deal with uncertainty by manufacturing a sense of security. This process allows us to become immune to the uncertainty in our stress environments. During the unprecedented uncertainty of COVID-19, I facilitated countless programs on how to deal with the stress of unpredictable financial and social issues.

> ## Manufactured security is the antidote to uncertainty.

This is really safety training for life. Taking the time to contemplate the "what ifs" of life may not be your regular practice, but thinking through and preparing for unpredictable challenges increases your ability to deal with them efficiently and productively. It can also lower your stress level now and during a crisis. Although security is an illusion because it doesn't prevent something bad from happening, by manufacturing the feeling of security you can reduce stress, think critically and creatively, and enjoy life.

For example, our family vacations usually involve sailing our 39-foot sailboat across Lake Michigan from the Wisconsin side to the Michigan shore. Traveling 75 to 100 miles in a day over water in a boat that goes about 7 miles per hour may not be everyone's idea of a good time, but we love it. The water of this Great Lake hovers in the 50-degree range, which means that falling into the water becomes a life-threatening incident very quickly as hypothermia sets in. As we sail across the lake, we are many miles and hours away from getting help in an emergency. By the time we reach the middle, it would take four or five hours for the Coast Guard to get to us.

People ask if sailing across the lake is dangerous. The answer is yes, there is an inherent danger, but we do our best to limit it. The lake is called an inland sea because it is unpredictable, and conditions can change quickly. Waves can reach the height of 12 feet. We keep a close eye on the weather and sea conditions. We always wear life jackets, and when the girls were little, they were tethered to the boat. Our biggest fear, what is most unpredictable, is that someone will fall overboard. In the cold water, falling in can be a life-threatening event if we can't get to the person and get them back on board within about ten minutes.

So, how do we manufacture security so that we feel confident enough to sail across the lake?

My husband and I spend quite a bit of time thinking through how to rescue the person overboard and get them back on the boat. We've invested in equipment to allow us to be successful, including alarm systems in our life jackets that will alert us if one of us goes overboard and send a signal back to the boat with the location. We also have a block and tackle system to hoist someone out of the water and up six feet to get them back aboard. Crew overboard drills with our family and our racing crew are essential so that we can react quickly and use the equipment properly.

Stress Detour
Already feeling secure?
Skip ahead to Section 4 to learn how to
protect yourself from the physical damage
caused by stress.

We continue to think about what could happen and what we would do to address that issue. This "what if" process reduces our stress because we feel prepared. We've trained our brains to react as if someone falling overboard is predictable.

None of this equipment or practice will prevent someone from falling overboard. It does, however, increase our ability to deal with the situation and prevent it from becoming a life-threatening event. This manufactured security allows us to move forward confidently.

While you may never enter a manhole or cross a Great Lake on a sailboat, we all face uncertainty. The process of thinking through the steps to manufacture security is the key to responding with confidence to uncertainty rather than triggering a sometimes paralyzing stress reaction.

The next chapter has an exercise to help you do just that.

Chapter 7

MANUFACTURING SECURITY

Stress-Proof Exercise

Manufacturing Security Exercise

This exercise leads you through a process to explore thoroughly the source of uncertainty, the possible outcomes, what is necessary to control the outcome, and the behaviors required to practice responding rationally rather than emotionally. Over the years, I've helped people work through a variety of issues using this tool. Some of the concerns include:

- What if I lose my job?
- What if I don't have enough money to retire?
- What if I repeat the mistakes of my parents with my own children?
- What if this illness is fatal?
- What if my relationship falls apart?
- What if I don't get promoted?
- What if I quit?

Planning for the moments we dread most is often the key to stopping the loop of anxiety and starting to work rationally. The Manufacturing Security Exercise is a tool to help us get past the fear caused by our brain's reaction to uncertainty, begin to think critically, and move forward toward success and vitality.

The Manufacturing Security Exercise

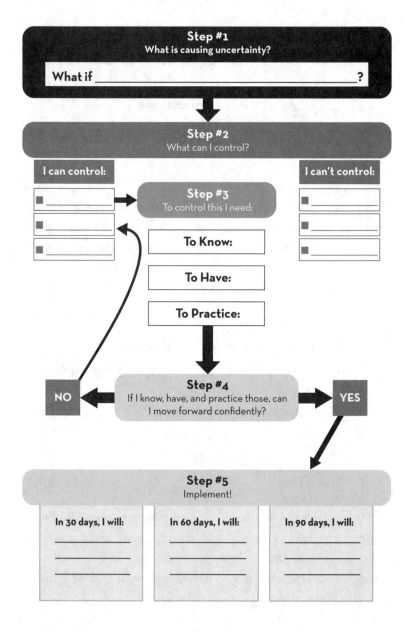

Step #1
What is causing uncertainty?

What if _____?

Step #2
What can I control?

I can control:
- ■ _____
- ■ _____
- ■ _____

Step #3
To control this I need:

To Know:

To Have:

To Practice:

I can't control:
- ■ _____
- ■ _____
- ■ _____

NO

Step #4
If I know, have, and practice those, can I move forward confidently?

YES

Step #5
Implement!

In 30 days, I will:
_____
_____
_____

In 60 days, I will:
_____
_____
_____

In 90 days, I will:
_____
_____
_____

There are five steps to manufacturing security:

1. Identify the cause of uncertainty.
2. Clarify what you can control and what you can't.
3. Examine what you can control.
4. Evaluate the level of security.
5. Implement your manufactured security plan.

The graphic on the previous page shows the five-step flow of this exercise.

I use crew-overboard drills as an example of how to manufacture security because, in essence, you are participating in a "life-overboard" recovery procedure.

Step #1: Identify the cause of uncertainty.

Ask yourself a "what if" question about the unpredictable condition causing uncertainty. Make your question as specific as possible. If you have several issues causing uncertainty, go through the Manufacturing Security Exercise for each one separately.

What if:

_____

_____

Example:

What if someone falls off our boat?

Step #2: Clarify what you can control and what you can't.

List what you can control about the unpredictable condition causing uncertainty in one column and what you can't control in the other.

I can't control:

_____

_____

_____

_____

I can control:

_____

_____

_____

_____

Example:

I can't control:

- Waves
- Wind
- Water temperature
- Storms
- Injuries

I can control:

- The equipment we have to get back to someone who fell overboard
- The equipment we have to get someone back on board the boat
- The equipment we have to keep someone on the boat
- How well we use the equipment
- How well we pay attention to the weather

Step #3: Examine what you can control.

What could you know, have, or practice to be able to control the things you listed in the first column? Start with just one of the things you can control.

To control:

_____

I need to know:

_____

_____

_____

_____

I need to have:

_____

_____

_____

_____

I need to practice:

_____

_____

_____

_____

Example:

To control: The equipment we have to get back to someone who fell overboard

I need to know:

- How to mark the spot the person fell in
- How to prepare the boat to turn around and get back to the person
- How to navigate to the person who may be moving with the waves and wind
- How to see the person in dark and/or stormy conditions

I need to have:

- A sensor attached to our life jackets that sends a signal if someone goes in the water
- A system to quickly stow the sails and get turned around
- A GPS navigation system that will receive the signal from the sensor and automatically create a track to follow to the person's current location
- Lights attached to our life jackets that spring up two feet above our heads and turn on automatically.

I need to practice:

- Using all of the equipment in crew-overboard drills. Every crew member needs to know how to use all of it and the procedures to follow.

Step #4: Evaluate the level of security.

If you knew, had, and practiced what you identified in Step #3, would this make dealing with any of the things you can't control more predictable? Does it manufacture enough security for you to confidently move forward in those uncertain conditions?

- If YES, great—move on to Step #5.
- If NO, complete Step #3 for the next thing you can control from the column in Step #2. If you have completed Step #3 for all of the things you listed in Step #2, you need to identify other things you can control. Sharing this exercise with someone else or seeking input from someone who has experienced a similar challenge or has expertise in the topic area can be very helpful.

Step #5: Implement your manufactured security.

The process of thinking through what you would need to manufacture security in the face of uncertainty may be enough to reduce your level of stress. Sometimes once we think through it, the situation seems more predictable, less risky, and less stressful. More often, however, we need to DO something different to break the cycle of stress. We need to actively prepare our brains to treat the source of uncertainty as predictable.

I am a firm believer that when you write something down, you are more likely to do it. The final step in this process is to identify what you will do in the next 7, 30, 60, and 90 days to build your sense of security. It is likely not possible to implement all of the things you identified in Step #3 at one time. Pick one and set a plan in motion.

In 7 days I will:

_____

_____

_____

_____

_____

_____

_____

Example:

In 7 days, I will identify the equipment we need.

In 30 days, I will:

_____

_____

_____

_____

_____

_____

_____

_____

Example:

In 30 days, I will research and order the equipment we need.

In 60 days, I will:

_____

_____

_____

_____

_____

_____

_____

_____

Example:

In 60 days, I will install the equipment and learn how to use it.

In 90 days, I will:

_____

_____

_____

_____

_____

_____

_____

_____

_____

Example:

In 90 days, I will:

- Develop a crew-overboard procedure and share it with the crew.
- Schedule a crew-overboard practice session.
- Review the success of the practice session and schedule more if necessary.

The next chapter provides strategies to use the discoveries made in this exercise to build a lasting sense of security.

Chapter 8

PRACTICING MANUFACTURED SECURITY

Stress-Proof Skill

Combat uncertainty by manufacturing security.

Manufactured security is a process, not a silver bullet.

Knowing what you need to have, know, and practice to move forward is essential, but you may need reminders and strategies along the way, like Morgan:

Morgan looked over to where Quinn used to sit. The empty desk was a daily reminder of the last round of "operational resource alignment" that eliminated Quinn's position. Morgan used to think their department was safe from layoffs, but that didn't seem to be true, and he is worried about his own future. Only seven years from retirement, Morgan worries the entire department might be eliminated. The kids are out of the house now, but do he and his wife Sally have enough money saved to make it through those pre-retirement years if he isn't working here? Can he find another job? What about insurance—can he get on Sally's plan at work? If he didn't get his act together soon and start producing better results at work, he might just get fired instead of being "realigned."

A few weeks ago, Sally's office had a program on leadership in crisis and change, and she brought home an exercise they both found useful in thinking through what they'd need so that being laid off wouldn't be a disaster. "We have enough," he says to himself as he stands and picks up his laptop. Relocating to an empty conference room, he repeats, "We have enough," to himself and settles into work.

As shown in Morgan's story, information alone can reduce stress. Below are five additional strategies for cultivating a sense of real security and generating lasting stress reduction:

1. Notice and accept the natural reaction to uncertainty.
2. Create a security talisman.
3. Disconnect from the source of uncertainty.
4. Behave your way to success.
5. Create artifacts of growth.

Strategy #1: Notice and accept the natural reaction to uncertainty.

Staring at a blank computer screen can be a big clue that you are experiencing a stress reaction to uncertainty, just as I did when I sat down to write this section. When you are robbed of critical thought or creativity or are just plain paralyzed by thoughts of what could happen, recognize this as a very natural response to the unknown.

My lack of focus and difficulty forming a decent paragraph resulted because the emotional part of my brain was busy thinking about whether my daughters could find their way at college. Morgan's low productivity was caused by a constant worry about the future of his job. Don't beat yourself up for having a natural reaction; you aren't a bad person, a lousy time manager, or lazy—you are stressed. Notice your stress reaction, and decide to take steps to address it.

Strategy #2: Create a security talisman.

A talisman is like a lucky charm. It is a touchstone that can ward off evil or bring good fortune. Can it really prevent bad things from happening? Maybe not, but carrying it makes you feel more confident in your ability to weather whatever comes along. Morgan's statement, "We have enough," is a talisman. The small statement reminds him of the work he and Sally did to prepare for the worst outcome of losing his job. On the boat in a big storm, I say to myself, "We have practiced for this." Whether your talisman is something you repeat to yourself or a physical object you hold or carry, it is critical to identify something that reminds you to feel confident.

Strategy #3: Disconnect from the source of uncertainty.

Thoughts about the source of uncertainty trigger stress. Section 4 of this book describes how to shut down the flow of cortisol by disconnecting from the source. For me, this was critical to shut down thoughts about the girls in order to get back to work on this book.

Fortunately, we had just finished sailboat racing season, which meant I had all sorts of yummy data to crunch. I can spend hours examining the results of moving boats to different divisions to create the fairest groupings.

Clay wonders what could possibly be so interesting about racing data, but I genuinely enjoy looking at the numbers, coming up with new questions, and then finding the answers. While I'm crunching away, I'm not thinking about our daughters. Then, when my head is clear, I'm able to return to my work with a renewed ability to focus. For Morgan, changing his environment is critical so that he can disconnect from the source of his uncertainty. Physically moving away from Quinn's desk removes a trigger for his thoughts about losing his job.

Changing locations, taking a quick walk to clear your head, or doing something mentally engaging can be the key to disconnecting from the source of uncertainty and moving forward.

Strategy #4: Behave your way to success.

My dad was a psychologist and would often talk about behaving your way to success. This entails going through the appropriate actions and doing them, even when it doesn't feel like you can, until they become more natural and intrinsically supported.

After struggling even to begin this section, finally I just did it anyway. It worked—you are reading this. I behaved my way into writing.

Whether you are practicing the behaviors you identified in Chapter 7 or simply going through the motions of important tasks until they begin to feel more natural, what you do changes how you feel.

The timer on your phone can be your best friend in this practice. On difficult days, I often function in 10-, 15-, or 30-minute segments. With writing, I just decide to write and commit to doing it regardless of how I feel, based on advice from my writing and speaking mentor Chris Clarke-Epstein. She is a big believer in writing with a pen and paper (or these days on a Rocketbook) because of the physical nature of the behavior. It feels different than typing on a keyboard. Even if I write, "This feels stupid. There is no way this is going to work," it works. That's because I'm performing the right behavior, which becomes more natural the longer I do it. Eventually, I become more engaged in the activity, and I make real progress as creativity and critical thought begin to flow.

Who's Who in the Book?
Check out more information about Chris Clarke-Epstein on page 308.

The same is true for you. What behavior will get you moving forward confidently?

Strategy #5: Create artifacts of growth.

Jake graduated at the top of his law school class and worked hard to develop a reputation in the legal community. He made partner in his firm and now wonders what is next. After years of defining success as reaching the next rung on the ladder, he has run out of rungs.

Is this all there is to his life? He doesn't feel engaged in his cases because there is nothing new to research or learn. Will it be this grind until he retires? Is his paycheck the only scorecard? Is it time to get a different degree? Try a different career? Jake's story is familiar to many high-achieving people who need to tackle challenges to feel fulfilled.

For Jake, the process of working toward the next goal is predictable. He knows how to do that. The unpredictability of being at the top of his career ladder creates uncertainty. His brain doesn't know how to prepare because there's no goal to reach toward, and it creates stress. His dissatisfaction and lack of interest in his job are symptoms of stress created by uncertainty.

Jake's experience is very common. Some people describe it as a mid-career crisis, a mid-life malaise, being stuck on the hamster wheel, the fear of better options, or the feeling that life is passing you by. However you describe it, this type of uncertainty can result in feeling depressed, disconnected from other people, and unmotivated to engage in work and life. Research shows that for many people, life satisfaction takes a dip at mid-life. It is common, but we don't often talk about it or share how to recover from it.

One of my favorite strategies to share with high performers dealing with mid-career uncertainty is the concept of artifacts of growth. These artifacts of growth can be professional or personal. Creating more rungs on the ladder of success makes people like Jake feel more secure. Reaching a goal is predictable. Jake could decide to learn to become a certified mediator or he could take up scuba diving. Both mediation and scuba diving have levels to complete. These levels are artifacts of growth; they recognize achievement.

My friend and fellow professional speaker, Thom Singer, serves as a great example of this. Thom is an expert in helping people and teams navigate the gap between potential and performance. One of his strategies is to "Try New Things." He lives that strategy in substantial ways. As a professional speaker and podcaster, Thom is comfortable talking, but he wanted to stretch into the hardest use of the spoken word: stand-up comedy. He wanted to see what he would learn and made a goal of doing 100 open mic nights over two years. Wherever he travels, he looks for the opportunity to go outside his comfort zone and perform a stand-up routine. This challenge has created opportunities to celebrate what he has learned after 25 performances, 50, 75, etc. These artifacts of growth recognize the expansion of his knowledge and skill.

Who's Who in the Book?
Learn more about Thom Singer on page 309.

Think about the artifacts of growth you can create. Will you try something new like Thom, dig deeper into your profession, or dive into a new hobby with levels to achieve?

Stress Detour
Having trouble disconnecting from the source of uncertainty?
Skip ahead to Section 5 to learn how to disengage to allow yourself to recover from stress.

Manufacturing security and practicing these strategies to support that security will reduce the stress caused by uncertainty. This, however, may not be enough to allow your cortisol level to come back to normal. The next sections deal with how to help your body eliminate cortisol and shut off the flow.

SECTION 4

Offsetting the Physical Impact of Stress

Chapter 9

CORTISOL IS THE PROBLEM

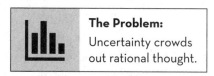

The Problem:
Uncertainty crowds
out rational thought.

High cortisol levels damage your heart.

Higigh cortisol levels eat away at physical health. Processing cortisol out of your body is essential to feeling better and protecting your health.

As we discussed in the first section, cortisol is the chemical your body releases when it senses stress. It is a natural, hardwired response. Prolonged stress, however, doesn't allow your cortisol level to return to normal and can damage your health, as Jerome discovered:

> *Jerome thought he was just tired. He has good reason to be. The last couple of years have been busy, having started a law firm with some friends. As the managing partner, his hours are long. He began experiencing spells of dizziness, during which he worried about passing out. He couldn't afford to look weak in front of clients—or worse, opposing counsel—so he went to the urgent care clinic. Of course, the doctor ordered a bunch of tests. Jerome figured she'd tell him to start exercising more and eat better.*

He wasn't expecting to be told he had blockages in two of the arteries in his heart. He couldn't believe it. He needed to have stents put in. He was only 47, and he needed a heart procedure. He really tries to eat well and get some exercise. He isn't overweight. Maybe all the long hours and stress took more of a toll than he thought?

Stress Detour
Is this sounding familiar?
If you've read *Stress-Proof Your Heart*, you are familiar with this concept and may have taken the quiz in the next chapter. If it has been more than 6 months, skip ahead and take the quiz again. If it was more recent, skip to Chapter 11, which has a few strategies you haven't seen yet.

Jerome is right to wonder about the impact of stress on heart health. High levels of the stress hormone cortisol cause thicker blood, higher blood pressure, and increased pulse, which all make the heart work harder. Prolonged high stress weakens the heart and doubles the risk of heart attack and stroke. Also, high cortisol levels are related to the increased risk of cancer and heart disease, along with other conditions of the endocrine and immune systems. Heart disease, however, is the number one cause of death for women and men of all ages. More people die of heart disease than the next seven causes, including all kinds of cancer combined.

Like Jerome, many relatively young people find themselves diagnosed with coronary artery disease, heart rhythm issues, or with high-risk factors such as elevated blood pressure, cholesterol, or blood sugar.

That is the bad news, but there is good news.

Keeping my heart healthy and protecting it from stress aren't abstract ideas for me—they're literally life-or-death skills. When I had a massive heart attack at the young age of 35 while 7 months pregnant with twins, I underwent five hours of open-heart surgery after delivering my daughters prematurely via emergency C-section. The surgeon repaired my heart, but a small part of it doesn't beat anymore. Even though my pregnancy caused the heart attack, I am at a higher risk of having another, so controlling my risk factors is essential. I can manage my diet and be physically active, but stress is an exponential multiplier of risk I simply can't afford. To reduce my heightened risk of having another heart attack, I've spent the 17 years since then honing practical and implementable strategies to manage stress for myself and the thousands of audience members and readers I reach each year.

> ## Your body is naturally equipped to process cortisol out of your system if you let it.

A stress-proof person more effectively processes cortisol, reducing it to normal levels, which in turn protects the heart, helps the person feel better, and even allows the brain to function better.

Stress-Proof Leadership Insight
Self-sacrifice won't improve your team's performance.
Read about this insight on page 259.

Stress is the Powerball of heart disease risk factors.

One of the most challenging things to explain is how heart disease risk factors don't just add up; they multiply exponentially.

Think about it like this: stress is the Powerball of risk factors. It makes your risk exponentially higher. This Powerball effect is your physical stress impact.

Cortisol isn't the enemy.

Life without the zing of excitement of cortisol would be boring. Stress-proof people use the cortisol reaction to respond to stressors (both good and bad) and then efficiently process it out of their bodies, like Jesse:

Jesse is an ER nurse in a busy metropolitan-area hospital. Near the end of a 12-hour shift, Jesse is tired, but he scrambles to meet the ambulances bringing patients from a multiple-car accident. Suddenly, he's not tired. With speed and skill, he meets the gurneys, triaging patients, and directing staff. In less than an hour, all the patients are stabilized and receiving treatment.

Jesse stands at the nurses' station, shakes out his arms, and takes a few deep breaths. He feels the tingly energy of the emergency draining from his body. He performed well, and he feels a sense of calm as he heads home. His hardwired cortisol reaction to the incoming patients made it possible to do his job, even though he was tired. The sense of "ahhhh" after the crisis has passed is the sign that his cortisol level is falling back to normal.

Learning to help your body process cortisol is essential to a long and healthy life.

How do you determine the physical impact of your stress or the size of your Powerball? The assessment in the next chapter enables you to do just that. Don't worry—in Chapter 11, you'll learn how to offset your physical stress impact by helping your body return your cortisol level to normal.

Evaluating the impact that stress creates on your physical health is essential to reducing it.

Stress Detour
Did you skip Chapter 2?
Pop back to page 27 and use the exercise to complete the next assessment.

The assessment in the next chapter determines the physical impact of your stress using the Stress Level Index from Chapter 2.

Chapter 10

HOW MUCH DAMAGE IS YOUR STRESS CAUSING?

 Stress-Proof Exercise

Physical Stress Impact Assessment

I developed the assessment in this chapter based on information from the American Heart Association and the American College of Cardiology. Thousands of clients and audience members have used this assessment to determine their personal risk of heart disease. You can find more information about heart health from these sources at StressProofResources.com.

Imagine you've been given 100 chances to live to the ripe old age of 97 in excellent health, with all of your faculties intact, and then pass away peacefully in your sleep.

Sounds great, right? Those chances are represented by circles on the worksheet on page 125. Risk factors for heart disease, including stress, take away some of those chances.

In this assessment, you'll find a series of questions about risk factors. As you answer the questions on the following pages, you will be instructed to cross off some of those circles, representing lost chances of having that long, healthy life.

Some risk factors, like stress, are risk multipliers, which means they exponentially increase the number of chances you may lose, so it is important to answer the quiz questions in order. The results of the later questions depend on your responses in the first sections.

After you complete the quiz, you will have an illustration of your risk of heart disease by evaluating three categories of risk:

- **Inherited risk factors:** There are certain risk factors we can't change; we are born with them. Age, gender, ethnicity, and family history all lay the foundation for our physical health and heart disease risk.

- **Internal risk factors:** These risk factors don't typically have symptoms, especially in their early stages, but they can drastically increase your chances of developing heart disease. These risk factors, such as high blood pressure, high blood sugar, and high cholesterol, need to be evaluated by a health professional.

- **Lifestyle risk factors:** Our activity level, our diet, our habits, how much we sleep, and how much we worry exponentially amplify our risk for heart disease. These are risk factors that we control and have the most potential to improve.

The results of the following assessment will help you identify steps you can take to offset the physical impact of your stress.

1. ## Inherited Risk Factors: Some risk factors are yours for keeps

Your Age and Gender:

Cross out all circles that apply to you.

Are you age 44 or younger?

Cross out **0** circles.

Are you using hormonal birth control such as the pill, ring, or patch (any age)?

Cross out **5** circles.

Are you a woman age 45–65 and still menstruating regularly?

Cross out **5** circles.

Are you age 45–65 and peri- or post-menopausal?

Cross out **7** circles.

Are you age 65 or older?

Cross out **10** circles.

Number of circles to cross out for your age and gender: _____

Your Ethnicity:

Cross out all circles that apply to you.

Is your family from Hawaii or India?

Cross out **10** circles.

Is your family from Mexico?

Cross out **10** circles.

Is your family from Africa?

Cross out **10** circles.

Is your family Native American or Native Alaskan?

Cross out **10** circles.

Number of circles to cross out for your ethnicity: _____

Your Family History:

Cross out all circles that apply to you.

Has your mother, father, or sibling been diagnosed with heart disease before age 60?

Cross out **10** circles.

Has a grandfather, grandmother, uncle, or aunt been diagnosed with heart disease before age 60 or died of a heart attack or stroke?

Cross out **10** circles.

Have you had a heart attack or been diagnosed with heart disease?

Cross out **20** circles.

Don't know your family history?

Cross out **5** circles.

Number of circles to cross out for your family history: _____

Total number of circles to cross out for your inherited risk factors: _____

Go to the worksheet on page 125 to record your inherited risk factor results like this:

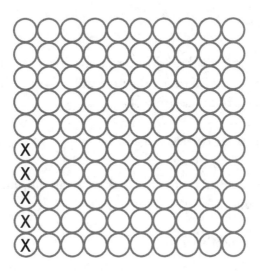

2. Internal Risk Factors: Some risk factors are silent

Your Blood Pressure:

Blood pressure measures how hard your heart needs to work to push your blood through the veins and arteries. The top number is the pressure during a heartbeat, and the bottom number is the pressure between beats.

For this quiz, we'll keep it simple and look at the top number.

Is your top number 119 or lower?

Cross out **0** circles.

Is your top number between 120 and 139?

Cross out **5** circles.

Is your top number between 140 and 159?

Cross out **15** circles.

Is your top number above 160?

Cross out **25** circles.

Number of circles to cross out for your blood pressure level:

_____

Your Cholesterol Level:

Cholesterol is a fatty substance that travels through the bloodstream and is essential to our health. "Good" cholesterol, high-density lipoprotein (HDL), carries our hormones and even keeps our skin supple. But too much cholesterol, especially low-density lipoprotein (LDL)—the "bad" kind— is a problem. Along the way, this "bad" cholesterol can deposit and sink into the walls of arteries, creating a buildup called plaque. Think of it as sludge forming on the inside of pipes.

Is your HDL:

Below 40?

Cross out **5** circles.

40 or above?

Cross out **0** circles.

Is your LDL:

Below 100?

Cross out **0** circles.

100 to 129?

Cross out **5** circles.

130 to 159?

Cross out **10** circles.

160 to 189?

Cross out **20** circles.

190 or above?

Cross out **30** circles.

Are your triglycerides:

149 or lower?

Cross out **0** circles.

150 to 199?

Cross out **5** circles.

200 to 499?

Cross out **10** circles.

500 or above?

Cross out **25** circles.

Number of circles to cross out for your cholesterol level:

_____

Your Blood Sugar:

For the sake of simplicity, this quiz uses the most common type of blood sugar test, the fasting plasma glucose test.

Is your fasting glucose level:

100 or below?

Cross out **0** circles.

101 to 125?

Cross out **10** circles.

125 or above?

Double the number of circles crossed out.

(Count the number of circles currently crossed out and then cross that number off again.)

Number of circles to cross out for your blood sugar level:

_____

Total number of circles to cross out for your internal risk factors: _____

Go to the worksheet on page 125 to record your inherited risk factors results like this:

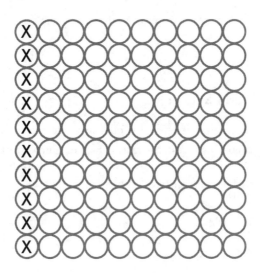

3. Lifestyle Risk Factors: Some risk factors are within your control

Waist-to-Hip Ratio:

Your body shape is a clue to your risk. The waist-to-hip ratio is a simple measurement—and, in many ways, a more helpful one than BMI—to determine how weight is distributed. Where you carry fat is important. The fat that is around the muscle and bone in your hips and legs is fine. Fat around the organs in your abdomen is dangerous.

Follow these easy steps to determine your waist-to-hip ratio:

1. Find a tape measure—the more flexible, the better.

2. Find your belly button.

3. Wrap the measuring tape around your waist at the level of your belly button.

4. Record your waist measurement below.

5. Find the fullest part between your hip bone and the top of your knees.

6. Wrap the measuring tape around that point.

7. Record your hip measurement below.

8. Divide your waist measurement by your hip measurement (WM ÷ HM).

9. The resulting number tells you the percentage of your waist measurement compared to your hip measurement. (For example, 0.7 is 70 percent.)

Waist Measurement (WM): _____

Hip Measurement (HM): _____

Waist-to-Hip Ratio: _____

Understanding Your Waist-to-Hip Results:

- Men: The healthy ratio for men is 1 or 100 percent. In other words, for men the hips and waist should measure the same. They should be straight at the torso rather than round.
- Women: The healthy ratio for women is 0.8 or 80 percent. In other words, for women the hips should be about 20 percent bigger than the waist. They should be curvy at the torso rather than round.

Waist-to-Hip	Impact on Risk
Men 1 or less Women 0.8 or less	Stays the Same
Men greater than 1 Women greater than 0.8	Doubles (Count the number of circles currently crossed out and then cross that number off again)

Number of circles to cross out
for your waist-to-hip results: _____

Smoking:

Smoking is a fast track to heart disease. People who smoke get heart disease decades before people who do not smoke.

Smoking	Impact on Risk
Nonsmoker	Stays the Same
Live or Work with Smoker	Doubles (Count the number of circles currently crossed out and then cross that number off again)
Smoker	Triples (Count the number of circles currently crossed out, multiply it by 2, and then cross that number off)

Number of circles to cross out
for your smoking results: _____

Total number of circles to cross out
for your lifestyle risk factors: _____

Go to the worksheet on page 125 to record your inherited risk
factor results like this:

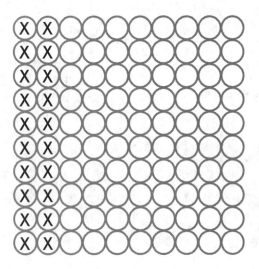

Your Stress:

Stress has an insidious impact on heart health. The physical changes in the body caused by stress magnify risk. Use the results of the Stress Level Index on page 30 to evaluate the impact on your risk.

Stress Level Index	Impact on Risk
Mild	Stays the Same
Moderate	Number increases by half (Count the number of circles currently crossed out divide by 2)
Critical	Doubles (Count the number of circles currently crossed out)
Acute	Triples (Count the number of circles currently crossed out and multiply it by 2)

Rather than crossing these circles out on the worksheet on page 125, write an "S" in them. The circles marked with an "S" indicate the physical impact of your stress.

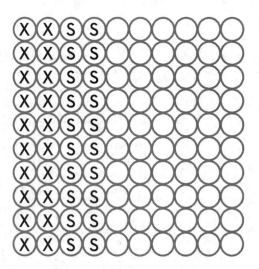

Number of circles in which to write "S": _____

Understanding Your Physical Stress Impact Results

Stress can rob you of years of a healthy, enjoyable life.

The Powerball effect of stress can amplify your risk of heart disease significantly, as Charlene learned:

"You need to get a handle on your stress," the doctor said. Charlene scoffed to herself, thinking that was easier said than done. As the regional sales director for a pharmaceutical company, she is always on the road. Keeping her team focused and up to date on changes is a non-stop struggle. She just lost one team member to another company, and finding a suitable replacement seems impossible.

But the doctor is right, and she knows it. She attended an American Heart Association event a few weeks ago and completed the speaker's quiz to figure out her risk of heart disease. Crossing out all the circles was kind of scary: her dad had a heart attack at 57.

Charlene's cholesterol is a little high, and truth be told, she isn't getting much exercise because she spends so much time in the car. As a result, she's carrying extra weight. Writing an "S" in 40 circles because her stress is so high was a wake-up call. The day after the event, she made an appointment to discuss her risk factors with her doctor. She knows something has to change.

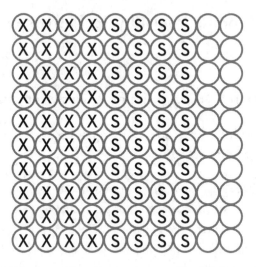

While Charlene's results may seem extreme, they really aren't unusual. Unless you know the problem and how big the problem is, it is tough to solve it. Most of us don't have tools to measure the physical impact of stress. Defining a problem is the best first step to solving it. This assessment offers that.

Use the worksheet on the next page with the assessment questions.

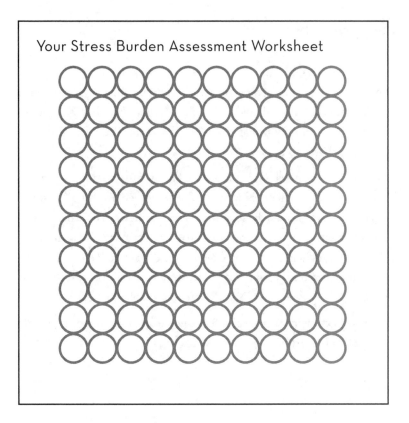

Your Stress Burden Assessment Worksheet

I've watched many people struggle with marking an "S" in their circles because they are shocked by the impact of their stress. But it is essential to be honest with yourself about your health.

How many of your circles have an "S" in them? This is the impact stress is placing on your physical health. Stress presses the fast-forward button on heart disease.

For example, if you have ten circles marked with an "S," you may develop heart disease ten years earlier. How much time and quality of life is stress taking away from you?

So, now what?

As you work to limit your risk of heart disease and stress-proof your heart, it is vital to partner with your health provider to take advantage of all the available tools. Like Charlene, the first step should be to make an appointment with your doctor to discuss all your risk factors and how to manage them.

While we can't change our age or family history, there are many ways to control other risk factors. Too often, we avoid going to the doctor to prevent ourselves from hearing bad news. The truth is, our bodies change over time, and with those changes our risk factors can tick slowly higher. Regular checkups and candid conversations with your doctor about all your risk factors can nip a problem in the bud instead of having to treat a life-threatening problem later.

The next chapter provides strategies to help your body process cortisol and return it to normal levels.

Chapter 11

PRACTICING PHYSICAL STRESS OFFSET

Stress-Proof Skill

Offset the physical impact of stress by effectively processing cortisol.

We all need to keep cortisol levels low to protect our hearts. If your risk is high, controlling cortisol levels is critical. For me, with my heart history, the strategies in this chapter are essential for keeping my heart strong and staying alive.

If we can bring our cortisol levels back to normal and keep them there most of the time, we can reduce the risk of heart disease down to the things we can't change, such as age and family history.

Help your body do what it is designed to do— get rid of cortisol!

Activities that direct your body to reduce cortisol and help process it out of your system offset the physical impact of your stress.

Ordinary activities, such as standing up and taking a quick walk once per hour, can significantly lower your cortisol level. Not only is this type of activity good for your heart, but it also has added benefits such as increased attention, fewer muscle aches from extended sitting, and better blood flow to the brain, which supports creativity and critical thought.

Use the zing of cortisol to get that project completed or assist your client in a time of need, and then use the eight strategies provided in this chapter to help your body efficiently eliminate the stress hormone:

1. Raise your heart rate.
2. Change your breath.
3. Drink enough water.
4. Keep your body fueled.
5. Change your view.
6. Improve your sleep habits.
7. Don't give up.
8. Recognize the signs of trouble.

Strategy #1: Raise your heart rate.

Any activity that raises your heart rate for a few minutes and then allows it to come back down can help reduce your cortisol level. For example:

There are two minutes left in the playoff game. If the team makes the field goal, they are going to the Super Bowl! Decked out for the home team, Jerome, Patricia, and Steve have been on their feet, cheering at the television throughout the hard-fought game. Jerry can feel his heart racing as the kicker lines up. Patricia is peeking through her fingers, hardly able to watch—the pressure is intense. Steve is rocking back and forth in his seat, willing the ball to go through the goalposts.

It does!

After high fives and cheering, all three fall back into their seats. Jerome takes a deep breath and is amazed by how great he feels. His pulse comes down, and his body settles.

That "ahhhh" feeling of your heart rate coming down is an indication that your cortisol level is coming down too.

So, could watching an exciting game actually reduce your stress? That may depend on who wins, but our emotions can undoubtedly raise our heart rate.

If at the end of the game you feel your heart rate settling down, you know that cortisol is coming down as well. This doesn't work, however, if the game or activity leaves you amped up and doesn't result in the "ahhhhh" feeling of your heart rate returning to normal. Harnessing the connection between heart rate and cortisol levels is a very effective way to process cortisol and offset the physical impact of stress.

Exercise is the antidote for stress.

Exercise conditions the heart and makes it work more efficiently. It lowers blood pressure and blood sugar. It clears bad cholesterol from your body and limits the number of triglycerides formed by converting the calories you eat into energy. It releases hormones that reduce pain and calm the brain. Exercise also helps purge your body of cortisol.

Engaging in aerobic exercise, which elevates and sustains the heart rate at 55 to 85 percent of your maximum heart rate for 20 to 30 minutes, several times per week can cut your risk of heart disease in half. For most of us, a brisk walk is enough to raise our heart rates into the aerobic zone.

Exercise's powerful combination of physical benefits and reduction of cortisol makes it a crucial method of stress-proofing your heart. It limits the adverse effects of cortisol and lessens your risk of heart disease. Not only will you feel better when you exercise, but the reduction of the cortisol in your system will help your brain work more effectively, too.

Nearly everyone gets some amount of activity during the day. The goal is to increase the amount of time you are moving. An obvious way to move more is to carve out 20 to 30 minutes of the day to walk, ride a bike, or do some other traditional cardiovascular exercise. This may work on some days but be difficult on others.

Luckily, it is not the only answer.

How do you fit more physical activity into your day?

If you can get to the gym or engage in traditional exercise a few days a week, great! What do you do on the other days or as an alternative? You can efficiently process cortisol with a combination of conventional exercise on some days, everyday activities, and other ideas in this chapter.

Use everyday activities.

Any activity that increases your heart rate, quickens your breath, and gives you a little "glow" counts as moderately intense cardiovascular activity.

Think about a 30-minute walk as the basis for comparison. Some household chores such as raking, mowing the lawn, or using a snow blower are equivalent in intensity. So, in other words, 30 minutes spent mowing the lawn (with a push mower, not a riding mower) is the same as taking a 30-minute walk.

Running is a more intense activity and will give you the same cardiovascular benefit in 15 minutes. Shoveling snow and hauling landscaping materials are more intense, as well. Doing less intense chores such as gardening, painting, and cleaning are also helpful ways to stay active, but it will take 60 minutes to receive the same benefit.

Everyday activities are a great way to meet your daily physical activity goal when there isn't time for more traditional exercise. The table below gives examples of a variety of activities at different levels of intensity. Balancing the intensity of your activity with the time in your schedule can help you meet your goal of improving your heart health and reducing your cortisol level.

Physical Activity Table

Intensity	Time	Walking/ Running	Sports
Low	60 minutes	2 miles @ 2 mph	golf, badminton, croquet, bowling, shuffleboard, table tennis, and softball
Moderate/ Low	45 minutes	1.75 miles @ 3 mph	volleyball, touch football, roller blading, rock climbing, & ice skating
Baseline Moderate	30 minutes	2 miles @ 4 mph Pushing stroller 1.5 miles@ 3 mph	doubles tennis, gymnastics, baseball, hockey, basketball, soccer, & cross country skiing
Moderate/High	20 minutes	1.5 miles @ 4.5 mph (run or fast walk)	lap swimming, singles tennis, & racquetball
High	15 minutes	1.5 miles @ 6 mph (run) stair climbing	singles tennis, bicycling 16 mph

Chores	"Gym" Activities	Seated Activities	"Fun" Activities
washing/waxing car, ironing, folding laundry, washing dishes	yoga, pilates, tae kwon do, free weights or machines	arm raises & circles, any household chores	frisbee, catch, batting practice
yard work (fertilizing, seeding, hand digging), cleaning house, woodworking, & painting walls	cardio w/ weights, resistance bands or balance ball	wheeling in wheelchair, arm excercises w/ weights/ bands	play in the pool, play in the snow
raking, sweeping, using push lawn mower or snowblower	water aerobics, cardio, dance (tap, ballet, ballroom) cardio, circuit, martial arts, Zumba	dynamic seated aerobics, fast wheeling in wheelchair	shooting baskets, kicking soccer ball, social dancing, tag, & bike riding (10-14 mph)
shoveling snow & digging holes	ski machine, elliptical, rowing machine	wheelchair basketball or rugby	
hauling rocks or other heavy items, & chopping down trees	jumping rope, high impact aerobics, spinning class, & step class		

A word of warning: Starting with a more intense activity can lead to symptoms such as lightheadedness, nausea, and even chest pain. Often, when people set a new exercise goal, they don't pay attention to their bodies and work out too intensely. It is a good idea to have a conversation with your doctor or a trainer about what level of intensity is right for you. When in doubt, start with a less intense activity. Also, keep in mind that jumping right into a high-intensity activity can cause injury. Allow your body to warm up.

Use chunks of activities.

Breaking your activity into 10- or 15-minute chunks may be more convenient on busy days. Try these ideas to take your heart rate up and your cortisol down:

- Take your dog for a 15-minute walk twice per day.
- Park farther away or take a lap around your building before you start work.
- Walk the halls at break time or lunch. (However, you must keep going. Encourage those who want to chat to walk with you!)
- When traveling, plan to walk 15 minutes between security and your gate and between the plane and baggage claim— you'll be good for the day.

Make the most of being on your feet.

Strap on a pedometer and count your steps (10,000 steps is equivalent to a 30-minute brisk walk). Any time you can make the pedometer click, you've done the equivalent of a step. Make the most of being on your feet by:

- Wiggling your hips while standing in line or brushing your teeth
- Pacing while talking on the phone

What works for you?

Think about ideas for working more ways to raise your heart rate into your day. Use the following prompts to write down some activities you can engage in:

What low-intensity activity could you do at the end of the day to help lower your cortisol level before bedtime (a walk around the neighborhood, tidying up around your home, or yoga, for example)?

_____

_____

_____

_____

What "screen time" activities are highly engaging and raise your heart rate (sports, suspenseful television programs, or interactive video games, for example)?

_____

_____

_____

_____

Which moderate- to high-intensity activities do you enjoy? Which one(s) could you work into your day more often?

When can you fit in a few extra steps or a little bit of activity?

Strategy #2: Change your breath.

When we are stressed, we take short, shallow breaths. Slowing down your breathing directs your body to lower cortisol levels. For example:

> *Stuck in traffic once again, Chantel feels her pulse rising. Remembering a tip from an employee wellness event, she flips on the radio*

and pulls up her "stuck in traffic" playlist on her phone. As Beyoncé starts singing about "All the Single Ladies," Chantel sings along at the top of her lungs. Not only is being stuck in traffic a bit more enjoyable with a soundtrack, but Chantel feels calmer and more energized as she finally pulls into the parking lot.

Changing the pattern of your breath feels good too. Singing is a great way to change the length and depth of breath and has been shown to act as a natural antidepressant. Most people feel calmer and more energized after singing. This means that blasting your favorite song and singing along while stuck in traffic is a great stress-reduction strategy!

Laughter works the same way. When we laugh, we disrupt our breathing pattern and release endorphins into the system, just like with singing. Watching a funny movie, talking with a witty friend, or surfing silly videos on your phone can be great ways to elevate your mood and reduce cortisol by changing your breath. (Do yourself a favor and google "Pancakey Wife Video"—you won't be sorry.)

Any activity that changes your breathing pattern works. This is why meditation and yoga are often suggested for stress reduction. Aerobic exercise can change your breath, too.

At an event for human resources professionals, an audience member shared a strategy to transition from work mode to home mode and back again. She has specific "walk-in" songs programmed. Singing along to the songs not only puts her in the right frame of mind, but it also sends her in calm and energized. Great idea!

Use the prompts below to identify opportunities to change your breath:

In the morning, when do you feel your breath shortening or your pulse rising?

_____

_____

_____

_____

How can you change your breath during those times?

_____

_____

_____

_____

During the workday, are there regular times you feel your breath shortening or your pulse rising?

_____

_____

_____

_____

How can you change your breath during those times?

_____

_____

_____

_____

When are your times of transition?

_____

_____

_____

_____

How can you change your breath during those times?

_____

_____

_____

_____

In the evening, when do you feel your breath shortening or your pulse rising?

_____

_____

_____

_____

How can you change your breath during those times?

_____

_____

_____

_____

Strategy #3: Drink enough water.

One of the biggest favors you can do for your body is to drink enough water. Being thirsty can cause stress and trigger bigger problems. For example:

The plane was hot and smelly. They'd been sitting on the tarmac for more than an hour, and Patricia wasn't feeling well. She shifted in her seat and pulled at her top and waistband, which all felt too tight. Taking her water bottle out of her bag, Patricia was frustrated to find it empty. She didn't have a chance to fill it this morning when she flew in for the meeting at the regional office. This had been a packed day with few breaks. There was barely time for lunch, and she didn't drink much during the day, either.

She took some deep breaths and tried to calm down. Why was her heart beating so fast? Suddenly, she felt like her heart was a fish flopping around in her chest. The woman in the seat next to her asked if Patricia was okay. Patricia just shook her head, and the kind stranger pushed the button to get the flight attendant's attention.

It turns out, Patricia was experiencing atrial fibrillation, the most common type of abnormal heart rhythm.

Patricia's story is an extreme example of the danger of dehydration. Staying hydrated also protects your heart and stops the stress of your body's reaction to dehydration from triggering a cortisol response. You can find out more about how dehydration triggers heart problems at StressProofResources.com.

How much water do you need every day?

Your body needs water to regulate temperature, digest food, eliminate waste, and keep your blood flowing. If your body doesn't get enough water, it will hold on to fat and your blood will thicken. If you have reached a plateau in weight loss or have trouble managing your blood pressure, pay attention to the amount of water you drink each day.

The bigger the body, the more fluid you need. Without the proper amount of water, your body doesn't function correctly. It is more than just dry skin or dry mouth—dehydration reduces your body's ability to flow. This can result in achy joints and muscles, high blood pressure, and reduced kidney function—and that's just the start of the list of possible issues.

A good rule of thumb to determine the minimum amount of water you should drink each day is to divide your weight (in pounds) by two. You should drink at least that number of ounces of water each day.

For example:

Weight: 150 lbs.

$150 \div 2 = 75$

This person should drink 75 ounces of water per day. Consult your doctor or registered dietitian nutritionist to figure out exactly how much water you should drink based on your health needs, exercise load, and climate.

Does it have to be water?

Well, no, but water is best for the majority of your fluid intake. Water doesn't contain anything more—no calories, no additives, nothing extra; it is just water.

If you don't like drinking plain water, you can dress it up with:

- Unsweetened herbal tea (hot or cold)
- A squirt of fruit juice
- Bubbles (carbonated water)

Other beverages can be used in moderation to fulfill your need for fluid:

- Unsweetened coffee is fine as some of your fluids, although it contains caffeine, but no additional calories. Limit it to three or four cups per day. Some people shouldn't drink caffeine at all. Talk to your doctor about how much caffeine per day is healthy for you.
- Milk works well for some of your fluid intake. The beneficial vitamins and minerals offset the added calories.
- Fruit juices carry quite a few calories and should be watered down or limited to a small glass per day.

Things you shouldn't count in your daily fluid intake:

- Soda: Treat soda as liquid candy—it is loaded with calories your body doesn't need and often can't use.
- Diet soda: High levels of sodium counteract your hydration efforts.
- Sports drinks: Unless you need to replace electrolytes because you have been profusely sweating for an extended period of time, you should not use a sports drink instead of water. Originally designed to aid athletes losing electrolytes through sweat, sports drinks have somehow become a casual beverage. Seriously, it isn't a "health drink"—stop it.

Are you getting enough water each day?

Keep track today and find out. Experiment with increasing your intake. How does it make you feel? Yes, you may have to visit the restroom more often, but a bit more walking doesn't hurt either!

Drink up!

 Use the prompts below to identify opportunities to increase your water intake:

How much water do you need each day?

Your weight (in pounds): _____

Divide your weight by 2 to find:

Number of ounces of water per day: _____

Thinking about your water intake in four time periods of the day can help you get enough.

Divide your number of ounces needed per day by 4 to find:

Number of ounces per time period: _____

 First Period: Start of day

How much water (or other beverages) do you drink before you start work?

_____ ounces

Is this more or less than the amount you need for each period? How many more ounces should you be drinking?

_____ ounces

Second Time Period: First three hours of work

How much water (or other beverages) do you drink in the first three hours of work?

_____ ounces

Is this more or less than that the amount you need for each time period? How many more ounces should you be drinking?

_____ ounces

🕐 Third Time Period: Second three hours of work

How much water (or other beverages) do you drink in the second three hours of work?

_____ ounces

Is this more or less than that the amount you need for each time period? How many more ounces should you be drinking?

_____ ounces

🕐 Fourth Time Period:
Transition from work to home

How much water (or other beverages) do you drink in the last hours of work and the first hour at home? (Keep in mind that many people need to limit fluid intake in the four hours before bedtime to sleep through the night.)

_____ ounces

Is this more or less than that the amount you need for each time period? How many more ounces should you be drinking?

_____ ounces

Strategy #4: Keep your body fueled.

Your body needs protein, water, carbohydrates, and fat to function correctly. Eating the right combination of foods doesn't have to be difficult. For example:

Steve isn't a big fan of vegetables; he'd rather grab a hamburger and fries at lunch. But after his last checkup, he knows some things have to change. He remembers a tip from an employee wellness webinar last week and looks at the menu for something colorful. There is a quinoa bowl with vegetables and chicken. That sounds colorful. As it turns out, it is pretty tasty, too.

Eating well provides the fuel to run your body and brain. Hunger increases stress and cortisol levels. Fueling your body doesn't have to be complicated. Ignore fad diets, celebrity lifestyles, and television doctors, and stick to a few simple strategies.

Your body uses the calories it needs for power and stores the rest as fat for later use. The trick is figuring out what to feed your body to fuel it well and not leave too much behind. Eating better doesn't require you to turn down everything you enjoy but rather to make good choices and seek out foods that will give you the fuel and energy to make it to the next snack or meal.

Eat fruits and vegetables.

Where's Your Proof?
Check out more information about this study on page 303.

The Centers for Disease Control says only one out of ten adults eats enough fruits and vegetables. I'm not suggesting that everyone become a vegetarian; however, we need to do better. The average adult should have at least five servings of fruits and veggies every day.

We can get caught up in the marketing around the "right" kinds of fruits and vegetables to choose, but I encourage you to keep it simple. I don't care if you choose the store-brand carrot or the locally sourced, organic one. Just eat a carrot!

Here are some ideas to integrate more fruits and veggies into your diet:

- For breakfast, blend up a smoothie. Choose whole-grain toast with peanut butter and banana slices or old-fashioned oatmeal with raisins and nuts.

- At lunch, choose something with lots of colors, such as a salad, stir-fry, or soup, rather than something brown or beige (e.g., a hamburger and French fries).

- During dinner, limit your portion of lean protein to about the size of a deck of cards and then fill the rest of your plate with vegetables and fruits.

- When snacking, grab a handful of trail mix with nuts and dried fruit. Try baby carrots and hummus or a good old-fashioned apple.

- For additional tips on how to get more fruits and vegetables, recipes, and information on eating better, visit the Academy of Nutrition and Dietetics website: EatRight.org.

Enjoy treats.

All food fits in a healthy diet, and too much of anything can be unhealthy. The goal is to enjoy a variety of food in moderation, even food containing sugar, fat, salt, or any other "bad" ingredients. Denying yourself the food you love—for example, chocolate—can derail good intentions because we can become focused on what we "can't" have or overeat other foods to compensate for feeling deprived. Have a treat every once in a while. Choose something indulgent and savor it.

Ask a real expert.

If you wonder about the right combination of foods you should be eating, don't rely on a nutritionist at the gym, a spa, or someone trying to sell a product. Instead, rely on a registered dietitian nutritionist (RDN). RDNs are the experts on nutrition and have the latest scientifically based information on healthy eating. Find one at EatRight.org/find-an-expert. You can find more nutrition resources at StressProofResources.com.

Pay attention to how you feel.

Your body has unique needs for fuel. Do you feel better eating three small meals per day and a couple of snacks? Skipping breakfast will slow down your metabolism and make it more difficult for your body to use the food you finally give it later in the day. As you experiment with adding more fruits and vegetables to your diet, notice how much protein and how many complex carbohydrates (whole grains, for example) you need to combine with them to keep your energy up and your hunger at bay until the next meal or snack.

Use the prompts below to identify opportunities to keep your body fueled:

What did you eat this morning?

_____

_____

_____

_____

How did you feel after you ate? Did you feel fueled for your activities?

_____

_____

_____

_____

Did you have a mid-morning snack? What did you eat?

_____

_____

_____

_____

How did you feel after you ate? Did you feel fueled for your activities?

_____

_____

_____

_____

Did you eat lunch? What did you have?

_____

_____

_____

_____

How did you feel after you ate? Did you feel fueled for your activities?

_____

_____

_____

_____

Did you have a mid-afternoon snack? What did you eat?

_____

_____

_____

_____

How did you feel after you ate? Did you feel fueled for your activities?

_____

_____

_____

_____

Did you eat dinner? What did you have?

_____

_____

_____

_____

How did you feel after you ate? Did you feel fueled for your activities?

_____

_____

_____

_____

Did you have a snack before bed? What did you eat?

_____

_____

_____

_____

How did you feel after you ate? Did you sleep well?

_____

_____

_____

_____

Strategy #5: Change your view.

Too often, our jobs keep us confined to a single place with a single view. Getting up and changing locations can stimulate the reduction of cortisol. Being outside 15 minutes per day and getting fresh air elevates mood and is an excellent way to reduce stress, get more vitamin D, and it may even change your perspective on a tough project or clear your head so you can work more efficiently. It is also great for your eyes. Spending time focusing at the same distance—say, working at a computer—makes your eyes tired and a little lazy. When you're outside, your eyes automatically focus on a series of distances to take in a new environment. This wakes up the brain and can help you refocus on work as well. Overall, nature is a guaranteed stress reducer—even looking at pictures or videos of nature works!

Strategy #6: Improve your sleep habits.

As I tell my audiences, "Sleep is the magic ingredient that makes everything else work."

You can exercise, eat right, and do everything your doctor says you should, but without enough good-quality, consistent sleep, it won't work. You may need to get creative like Charlene:

Charlene unpacked her "sleep kit" again. After three nights in three different hotels, she was ready to go home. Travel is just part of her job managing her sales team. She used to think she could catch up on sleep when she got back home, but it never really seemed to work. Her doctor told her sleep was the most important thing she could do to reduce her cortisol level. So, she put together a kit of things to help her sleep on the road. She has a sleep mask and a noise machine. Her son searched online and found a small folding fan to keep her cool. Her doctor suggested an herbal supplement to help her doze off. As silly as it seems, she packed a pillow, too—one that smells like home.

Poor sleep is also associated with anxiety and depression. Even more concerning, a recent lab-based research study conducted by the National Institutes of Health tied the lack of sleep with severe cognitive decreases. They found that if over two weeks, you are sleeping less than six hours per night, your cognitive and reflex abilities are the same as someone who didn't sleep for two full nights. This means that the majority of us are functioning at a decreased level most of the time!

Where's Your Proof?
Check out more information about this study on page 303.

Sleep is essential to a stress-proof heart for two reasons. First, sleep is the most efficient way to purge cortisol from your system. Second, the lack of sleep can cause the buildup of plaque.

Why is plaque terrible for your heart and brain?

Think of plaque as sludge forming on the inside of pipes. As plaque builds, the artery walls thicken, which narrows the space available for blood to flow. Ultimately, the buildup of plaque slows down the flow of blood. This reduced blood flow robs cells of the oxygen they need. This type of heart disease, atherosclerosis, is often referred to as "hardening of the arteries."

- When these plaque deposits are in arteries that supply the heart, it is called coronary artery disease, and it can cause a heart attack.
- When they form in the arteries that supply the arms and legs, it is called peripheral artery disease.
- When they form in the arteries that supply the brain, it can cause a stroke and is associated with Alzheimer's and dementia.

How much sleep do you need?

Six hours seems to be the bare minimum per night. Seven or eight is better, and more than nine appears to be too much.

Along with damaging your heart, a lack of sleep can rob you of efficiency and make any task harder. Your body will eventually force you to sleep. If you need a cup of coffee to keep going or find yourself dozing at your desk, it likely isn't because your job is boring—you are tired!

Are you getting enough sleep? Consider whether you experience any of the following:

- Do you find your mind wandering when reading a magazine article?
- Do you have trouble focusing your eyes when you are driving?
- Do you hit the snooze button several times each morning?
- Do you feel like the volume is turned up on your emotions?
- Do you forget appointments or important dates?

- Do you carry extra weight around your middle, no matter how much you count calories or exercise?
- Do you doze off while working on the computer or watching television?

If you answered "yes" to any of the above questions, you may not be getting enough sleep. If you are getting the sleep you need, you will wake up—without an alarm—feeling rested, refreshed, and ready to meet the day.

Tips for a better night's sleep:

- Limit caffeine past the early afternoon.
- Avoid using alcohol to induce sleep, as it causes interrupted and restless sleep.
- Be active for at least 30 minutes per day.
- Create a quiet, dark, and cool space to sleep.
- Turn off devices and avoid blue light screens as you wind down for bed.
- Pay attention to your bed, linens, and pillow. Small adjustments can increase comfort and bring better sleep.
- Talk with your doctor about any health conditions that may make sleep more elusive.
- Discuss any herbal or medical remedies that may ease chronic sleeplessness.
- You can find more resources for better sleep at StressProofResources.com.

Strategy #7: Don't give up.

Changing habits is hard and takes time and repetition before a new, healthier pattern feels natural.

The strategies in this section work well, but don't try to implement them all at the same time. Pick one, and then decide on a small, achievable daily habit you can perform for the next 100 days. If you stumble when trying to meet your goal, don't beat yourself up. If you miss a day, don't abandon your new healthy habit; start the next day again.

As I tell my clients, "Life is not about perfection. It's about moving in the right direction." There are days I take a step off the path when I eat cookies instead of lunch or stay up too late working on a project. As long as I get back on the right path, it will be okay. Don't give up on walking your path. Keep going, and know that even if you stumble, you'll make it.

Strategy #8: Recognize the signs of trouble.

Know when it is time to call 911.

One of my most popular YouTube videos answers the question, "Is it time to call 911?" So many people wait too long to seek help when they have a heart attack. The sooner you get help, the better the outcome will be. Don't drive yourself to the hospital. Calling 911 means you will start receiving life-saving treatment as soon as the first responders arrive.

Do you have:

- Unusual pain in your back, abdomen, shoulder, neck, chest, or jaw?
- Shortness of breath or trouble breathing (especially while sleeping or lying down)?
- Cold sweat?
- Racing heartbeat or the feeling of fluttering or missed beats?
- Pressure in your chest? Lightheadedness?
- Unusual and unexplained vomiting?

If you answered "yes" to ANY of these symptoms, it is time to call 911. These are signs you may be having a heart attack.

What does a heart attack feel like?

My heart attack started out feeling like heartburn. Because I was seven months pregnant with twins, heartburn for me wasn't unusual. But very quickly, things changed. I started vomiting, and my chest felt like my bra was five sizes too small. What at first seemed to be heartburn became so intense that I knew I was in trouble.

We all know what is normal for our bodies. Paying attention to unusual symptoms could mean the difference between life and death. This is especially important for women. Women's heart attack symptoms are often subtle and difficult to diagnose, even for professionals.

So, is that sharp, burning sensation in your chest caused by the pizza you just ate or a sign of something more serious?

Here are some ways to tell the difference:

- **Did exercise or physical activity bring on the symptoms?** If it did, this is a big clue to get help right away. It is time to call 911.

- **Is the pain stopping you from doing normal activities?** Heartburn can be uncomfortable, but a pain that distracts you from work or causes you to withdraw from activities should be evaluated by a medical professional quickly. It is time to call 911.

- **Do you have risk factors for heart attack?** High blood pressure, high cholesterol, high stress, being overweight, being sedentary, and having family members with heart disease are signs you may be more likely to be having a heart attack. It is time to call 911.

- **Did you eat something that upset your stomach?** If your tummy is usually upset 30 to 40 minutes after eating spicy or greasy food, chances are it is heartburn. But if you haven't eaten, or if what you ate doesn't usually cause stomach upset, then it is cause for concern. It is time to call 911.

- **Does antacid help?** Usually, the relief is immediate. If you take an H2 blocker such as Zantac or Tagamet, relief should come in 30 to 40 minutes. If the pain continues or gets worse, seek medical attention right away. It is time to call 911.

Pay attention to the signs your body sends. Even if you seek help only to find out that you have acid reflux, that is significantly better than ignoring symptoms of an actual heart attack.

Using the strategies in this chapter is beneficial in offsetting the physical impact of stress:

- Raising your heart rate.

- Changing your breath.
- Drinking enough water.
- Keeping your body fueled.
- Changing your view.
- Improving your sleep habits.
- Not giving up.
- Recognizing the signs of trouble.

However...

These strategies won't work if cortisol is constantly pumping into your system. For example, even if you try all of those tips, the stress chemical, cortisol, can make it difficult to fall asleep. As we discussed, sleep is essential to processing cortisol out of your body. One of the best things you can do to get more sleep is to disconnect from stress triggers in the two to three hours before bed.

Section 5 provides strategies to disconnect from the source of psychological stress so that you can recover from the toll of the stress in your environment.

SECTION 5

Recovering from Psychological Stress

Chapter 12

WHAT KEEPS YOU UP AT NIGHT?

The Problem:
Psychological stress keeps cortisol flowing.

Unlike physical stress, psychological stress often continues well after the stressful incident has passed.

L earning how to disconnect from the cause of stress and recover is an essential piece of stress-proofing. When we continue to think about a stressful situation or stay "revved up" about something, our cortisol level stays elevated. One of the frustrating symptoms of high cortisol levels caused by psychological stress is difficulty sleeping.

Derek rolls over carefully, trying not to wake his fiancée. Looking at the clock, he starts calculating how much sleep he will get if he starts now. It is 3:14 A.M., and the alarm is set for 6:00. Will less than three hours be enough? Should he just get up now and give up on the idea of sleep?

Maybe he could get ahead on the Mayfield project. He hasn't been able to make much progress since the Romero project is still requiring attention. What he needed was one more project manager on staff to take some of the load off. Sure, all of the growth and new business with the recent merger with another firm has been great, but why isn't leadership keeping up with the demands for good staff?

His boss doesn't have any answers, and she's worried about her own job after the merger is complete. Lack of sleep isn't helping anything. It seems like months since Derek has had a full night's sleep. If only he could shut off his brain for a while and stop thinking about all of the things that are stressing him out.

Shutting down the flow of cortisol allows your body to recover from stress.

Disconnecting from the cause of psychological stress is key to stopping the flow of cortisol and recovering from the impact of stress. The previous section's strategies for offsetting the physical impact of stress work only if cortisol has stopped pumping into the system.

Psychological stress reactions continue to pump cortisol into the body even when the stressor isn't present. This is why stress can keep us up at night. High cortisol levels make it hard to sleep, which leads to thinking about stressful things, which then pumps even more cortisol into the system. It can be a vicious cycle.

Your body needs to be able to recover from psychological stress, and this is where most stress management programs fail. One of the most exciting things I've learned is that addressing the psychological side of stress is not a one-size-fits-all solution.

Most stress reduction strategies tend toward quiet, contemplative activities such as yoga or meditation. These activities work well for some people, but for others, sitting quietly and concentrating on their breathing increases their stress because they can't stop thinking about their stressors.

We all have different needs for distraction, contemplation, engagement, social interaction, and solitude when it comes to stress recovery.

This was comically demonstrated while my husband and I were on vacation in Mexico, celebrating his 50th birthday. We traveled with five other adults to a resort that caters to scuba divers. I don't dive, but my husband, Clay, is enthusiastic about the sport, as were our fellow travelers. This interaction led to some fascinating insight on stress and relaxation.

When not diving, most of our group spent time lounging by the pool, with the iguanas (yes, actual iguanas). Being fair-skinned, I spent some enjoyable time by the pool, in the shade. Clay did not, however, have the staying power of the rest of the group. He enjoyed being an iguana for a while but then also needed to DO something. We took out the little sailboat, went for walks—coming and going from the pool.

One of our fellow travelers remarked to Clay, "You are always on the go. When are you going to relax?"

Here's the thing—he was relaxing.

Clay joked at dinner one evening, "I'm like a border collie: if I don't have something to do, I start chewing on things."

This is both funny and true. It is also an excellent description of how Clay relaxes. He needs something diverting him from thinking about the things that cause stress. Staying quiet and still provides him with too much time to think. Our vacations tend to be action-packed, but we've come to recognize that I need some "iguana time" along the way to get what I need to disengage and recover from stress—for example, sitting on the beach and watching the sunset, next to my wonderful husband.

How do you disengage?

Too often, we think of relaxation in only one facet: stillness. Meditation works for many "iguanas," but if you are a border collie at heart, it may cause more stress to try to be still. For border collies, distraction from stressors is essential.

Hobbies are excellent for reducing stress. My dad, for example, loved woodworking and spent hours in his garage workshop building, sanding, and finishing furniture, children's toys, and many gifts. The "busy hands/free mind" essence of these actions can reduce stress for many people.

Other people need highly engaging activities to reduce stress. Racing on an all-woman sailing crew, I saw this in action. All of us have demanding jobs, but running from one side of the boat to the other, working as a team to deploy sails and build speed, as well as laughing when things didn't go as planned reduced our stress because we were entirely focused on the task at hand. My guess is that all of us have some border collie tendencies, even though, like me, some of us need some contemplative iguana time too.

Your way of relaxing might not look the same as it does for your spouse, co-worker, or friend, but that is okay. Embrace your own style and make time for activities to support your stress reduction. When I was facilitating this exercise at an association conference, one audience member said she'd spend her Friday night organizing her closet—and some of the rest of the audience members booed her. Not cool! If that is what allows her to recover, who are we to judge? Clutter and disorganization often increase stress. Putting things in order can be doubly effective in recovering from stress by both solving a problem and also disengaging from other stressors.

Like me, people often fall somewhere in the middle between border collie and iguana. The trick is to identify—and then give yourself permission to make time for—activities that will allow you to disengage and recover from psychological stress.

> Our bodies are amazingly adaptable, but they require time to rest and recover from stress.

Jennifer finishes the dinner dishes as her husband, Daniel, puts the kids to bed. After kissing each of the girls good night and having a quick conversation with Daniel, she sits down and opens her laptop. Managing customer relations for a global company seems to be a 24-hour-per-day job. She finishes reviewing the social media response report and hopes nothing controversial develops overnight. She calls her co-lead overseas to put the finishing touches on the report for this quarter. Hanging up, she glances at the treadmill taunting her from the corner. Not tonight, she is just too tired, and she has at least another hour of work before she can get some sleep.

All she really wants is to be in her bed. She loves her bed. Jennifer's definition of a great day would be staying in bed, having people bring her food, and never having to take care of anything other than the television remote. But she can't do that, of course. A whole day in bed would be lazy, a waste of a day.

But what if that is exactly what Jennifer needs to recover? As an iguana, Jennifer needs quiet time and sleep to allow her to physically and psychologically recover from stress. Too often, we deny ourselves the very thing that would be most effective in our stress recovery.

Just like any complex machine, if overworked without proper maintenance, our bodies will break down. In that sense, stress is neither good nor bad; it is simply causing a natural chemical reaction in the body. Stress recovery takes time, and our busy lives often get in the way of taking the time necessary to allow the body to process and reduce the stress chemical cortisol. Making the time for recovery is essential to becoming immune to the stress in your environment.

The next chapter walks through a fun quiz to determine your stress recovery personality, which will enable you to pinpoint the type of activities that will best help you process cortisol out of your system.

Chapter 13

WHAT IS YOUR STRESS RECOVERY PERSONALITY?

Stress-Proof Exercise

Physical Stress Impact Assessment

Are you an iguana or a border collie?

Understanding and embracing the type of activities you need to disengage from stress—your Stress Recovery Personality—is essential to stress-proofing.

Some of us play for just one team. We are on Team Iguana or Team Border Collie. Others mix it up. The trick to stress recovery is making sure your needs are being met.

The following quiz will help you determine if you are an iguana, a border collie, or somewhere in between.

Use the answer sheet on the next page to mark your answers to the quiz questions, or take the quiz online at StressProof.Life.

1.	☐ A	☐ B	☐ C	☐ D	☐ E
2.	☐ A	☐ B	☐ C	☐ D	☐ E
3.	☐ A	☐ B	☐ C	☐ D	☐ E
4.	☐ A	☐ B	☐ C	☐ D	☐ E
5.	☐ A	☐ B	☐ C	☐ D	☐ E

1. Imagine it is a Tuesday night. You miraculously have left work at 5:30 and have two hours of free time. If you have children, Mary Poppins is in town and will put them to bed. You don't have to finish any work, and you don't have to make dinner for anyone if you don't want to. How would you like to spend that time?

Would you like to:

A. Sleep?

B. Watch your guilty-pleasure television program?

C. Cook dinner and have a glass of wine with your partner?

D. Do a project around the house, tidy up, or organize something?

E. Go to the gym and get your sweat on?

2. It is Friday night and—again—if you have children, Mary Poppins has taken them to her house for a sleepover. How would you like to spend that time?

Would you like to:

A. Binge-watch something?
B. Go to a bookstore, art supply shop, or other "poke-around" location?
C. Attend a play or movie?
D. Have dinner out with friends?
E. Go somewhere with music, friends, and dancing?

3. It is Saturday afternoon, and it is a beautiful day. How would you like to spend that time?

Does your day include:

A. A hammock, a book, and a refreshing beverage?
B. A computer, Wi-Fi, and coffee?
C. Paints, crafts, or carpentry?
D. Dirt, plants, and a little sweat?
E. Sneakers, athletic clothing, and maybe a little competition?

4. It is late Sunday morning and another beautiful day. Where would you spend the next few hours?

Are you:

    A. Still in bed sleeping?

    B. Doing the Sunday crossword puzzle?

    C. Out for brunch?

    D. In the park with friends or your dog?

    E. Out biking or exploring?

5. On vacation, what type of activity would you most enjoy?

Would you:

    A. Find a quiet spot to read, rest, and recover?

    B. Use a guide to find the best places for local food?

    C. Take a walking tour of a new town?

    D. Hike to a secluded waterfall?

    E. Zip-line in a remote area?

Understanding Your Stress Recovery Personality Quiz Results

Your Stress Recovery Personality indicates the type of activity most likely to lower your cortisol level by allowing you to disengage from the source of stress. Some people need highly engaging activities, while others benefit from being more contemplative.

Where are most of your marks on your Stress Recovery Personality Quiz Results?

If most of your answers are A, you are on Team Iguana.

1.	☒ A	☐ B	☐ C	☐ D	☐ E
2.	☒ A	☐ B	☐ C	☐ D	☐ E
3.	☒ A	☐ B	☐ C	☐ D	☐ E
4.	☐ A	☒ B	☐ C	☐ D	☐ E
5.	☒ A	☐ B	☐ C	☐ D	☐ E

To recover from stress, iguanas seek calm environments and more contemplative activities. Creative hobbies and thought-provoking activities are useful distractions from stress.

Try activities such as:

- meditating
- taking quiet walks in nature
- drawing
- watercolor painting
- model building
- photography
- doing puzzles
- tracing genealogy
- playing chess

- reading
- singing/playing music for your own enjoyment
- collecting stamps or coins
- studying astronomy
- knitting
- sewing
- crocheting
- quilting
- jewelry making
- floral arranging
- watching television
- scrapbooking
- visiting museums

If your answers are clustered toward the left (mostly Bs and Cs, with an A or two), you are an iguana with border collie tendencies.

1. ☒ A	☐ B	☐ C	☐ D	☐ E
2. ☐ A	☒ B	☐ C	☐ D	☐ E
3. ☐ A	☐ B	☒ C	☐ D	☐ E
4. ☐ A	☒ B	☐ C	☐ D	☐ E
5. ☐ A	☒ B	☐ C	☐ D	☐ E

The most effective stress recovery activities will occupy the brain and allow you to create calm and recover from things causing you stress. Try activities such as:

- woodworking
- car restoration
- archery
- pool/billiards
- cooking
- baking
- learning a new language
- card playing
- homebrewing/winemaking
- computer programming
- gaming
- bird watching
- practicing yoga
- storytelling
- shopping
- antiquing
- binge-watching television
- scrolling social media
- going to the movies
- going to the theater
- going out with friends
- trivia contests
- ballroom dancing
- gardening

- camping
- fishing
- bowling
- magic
- writing/blogging
- volunteering
- singing/playing with other people
- metal detecting
- beekeeping
- studying meteorology
- caring for animals
- playing board games
- participating in a book club
- traveling by train or car
- kite flying
- biking
- golfing
- visiting zoos
- sport coaching or officiating
- fantasy sports
- wine tasting
- cooking classes
- weightlifting
- watching sports with friends
- service groups or clubs
- listening to music
- going to shows—auto, home and garden, boat, sports, etc.

If your answers are mostly Cs, you are on Team Iguana-Collie.

1.	☐ A	☒ B	☐ C	☐ D	☐ E
2.	☐ A	☐ B	☒ C	☐ D	☐ E
3.	☐ A	☐ B	☐ C	☒ D	☐ E
4.	☐ A	☐ B	☒ C	☐ D	☐ E
5.	☐ A	☐ B	☒ C	☐ D	☐ E

Many of us shift between iguana and border collie depending on the situation. In some moments, you may choose a calm, contemplative activity, and in others, an active, engaging activity will serve you better. Choose activities from the other lists to fit your needs.

If your answers are clustered to the right (mostly Cs and Ds, with an E or two), you are a border collie with iguana tendencies.

1.	☐ A	☐ B	☐ C	☒ D	☐ E
2.	☐ A	☐ B	☒ C	☐ D	☐ E
3.	☐ A	☐ B	☐ C	☒ D	☐ E
4.	☐ A	☐ B	☐ C	☐ D	☒ E
5.	☐ A	☐ B	☒ C	☐ D	☐ E

Your most effective stress recovery activities are highly engaging and allow you to be distracted from things causing you stress. Try activities such as:

- geocaching
- running
- practicing martial arts
- hiking
- sailing
- kayaking
- canoeing
- hunting
- backpacking
- dancing
- swimming
- doing improv
- performing music/singing
- going to rock concerts
- social dancing
- home improvement/repair
- battle reenactment/LARPing/cosplay
- organizing
- playing ping pong
- traveling by motorcycle
- horseback riding
- visiting amusement parks
- engaging in community activism
- entertaining

- acting
- playing frisbee golf

If most of your answers are E, you are on Team Border Collie.

1.	☐ A	☐ B	☐ C	☐ D	☒ E
2.	☐ A	☐ B	☐ C	☐ D	☒ E
3.	☐ A	☐ B	☐ C	☒ D	☐ E
4.	☐ A	☐ B	☐ C	☐ D	☒ E
5.	☐ A	☐ B	☐ C	☐ D	☒ E

The most effective stress recovery activities are active and allow you to be distracted from things causing you stress. Exercise, highly engaging hobbies, and other high-octane activities are your best bet. Try activities such as:

- playing paintball
- rock climbing
- mountain climbing
- running marathons
- flying
- sailboat racing
- fencing
- adventure racing
- playing team sports
- skiing/snowboarding

- doing parkour
- zip-lining/bungee jumping
- surfing
- windsurfing
- playing ultimate frisbee
- scuba diving

Ultimately, you need to give yourself permission to make the time for activities that allow you to disengage from thoughts about the source of your stress so that your cortisol level can come down.

Make the most of your stress recovery activities.

Activities that combine disconnection and one of the strategies from Section 4 to process cortisol out of your body are especially beneficial. For example, many of the activities listed under each Stress Recovery Personality Type involve movement, raising the heart rate, or changing your view. Including these types of activities can be very effective in limiting the impact of stress you can't control.

I've identified two other factors that can increase the potency of stress recovery activities:

- Social interaction
- Service

Social interaction.

We all have different social needs. Some of us enjoy jumping and singing in a huge crowd at a concert, while for others that is horribly uncomfortable. Some of us who work on our own, like me, lack a sense of belonging to a team and desire interaction. Others need a break from people and seek some solitude. Whether you choose to sit quietly by yourself and read or join a book club, if your stress recovery activity also meets your needs for social interaction (or the lack of interaction), you've increased the potency of that activity.

Service.

Doing something to benefit others takes the focus off of ourselves and can often reset our perspective. Research indicates that helping behavior may "undo" negative emotions and make us feel good. Of course, volunteering can become overwhelming and cause stress too. Reasonable service—performing helping behavior that is not overwhelming in terms of time or effort—that also allows you to disconnect from the source of stress adds to the potency of that activity.

The highest-potency stress recovery activities combine all four factors:

- Disconnection from stressors
- Offsetting the physical impact of stress
- Social interaction
- Service

Clay and I volunteer for Hunger Task Force, which provides a safety net of emergency food to a network of local food pantries and meal programs in our area. One of my favorite jobs is putting together stock boxes that are delivered to qualifying senior citizens in our community.

The work is fast-paced, and I don't think of anything other than the task at hand, so it allows me to disconnect from my stressors. We are packing about 40 pounds of food into each box, so the work is physical. Each person is responsible for placing a particular product in a specific spot in each box so the boxes are balanced for lifting. The teamwork required suits my need for social interaction. Finally, the two-hour commitment fits my schedule easily and feels great.

Think about the activities that can have the most impact on your stress recovery.

What is your Stress Recovery Personality Type?

_____

_____

_____

_____

Think about the type of activities you could incorporate into your day to disengage and recover from psychological stress.

Before work, what could you do to start your day to disengage from psychological stress?

_____

_____

_____

_____

At midday, what could you do to disengage and refocus?

_____

_____

_____

_____

As you transition from work to home, what activities could you include to recover from psychological stress?

_____

_____

_____

_____

As you transition to bedtime, what type of activities will allow you to disengage from psychological stress and lower your cortisol levels for sleep?

_____

_____

_____

_____

What high-potency activities could you incorporate on a weekly or monthly basis?

_____

_____

_____

_____

Chapter 14

PRACTICING STRESS RECOVERY

Stress-Proof Skill

Recover from psychological stress by disconnecting from the source.

Practicing stress recovery goes beyond identifying what works best to disconnect from stressors. It requires recognizing the signs of high stress, being proactive in stress recovery, and actually doing something to allow for recovery.

Below are six strategies for psychological stress recovery:

1. Recognize your need for stress recovery.
2. Sniff out contagious stress.
3. Be proactive rather than reactive.
4. Sip media, don't gulp.
5. Celebrate all victories.
6. Know when enough is enough.

Strategy #1: Recognize your need for stress recovery.

Some days are easier than others. On the more difficult days, recognizing the symptoms of increased stress is important. Pay attention to the signs of your stress level rising, such as:

Physical signs:

- headaches or migraines
- tense muscles
- stomach upset
- decrease in sex drive, more-painful-than-usual periods, or impotence
- faster-than-normal heart rate
- loss of appetite
- trouble sleeping

Behavioral signs:

- eating more than usual
- drinking or taking drugs to "take the edge off"

Cognitive signs:

- muddled thinking
- forgetting details or appointments
- indecision

- making unusual mistakes
- lack of focus
- poor decision-making

Emotional signs:

- out-of-character emotional responses
- feeling anxious
- finding little joy in things you used to enjoy
- constant worry

When you notice the signs of psychological stress, make a special effort to allow yourself to recover. Go back to the list of activities that are likely to be useful to you in Chapter 13 and make it a priority to disengage from stress.

Strategy #2: Sniff out contagious stress.

Stress is contagious, and a secondhand reaction to stress is hardwired.

Regina scurried into the office, hoping she wasn't going to lose the daily game of workspace roulette. No one wants to work near Marti, whose constant sighing, groaning, pen slamming, and discontented muttering were more than just distracting. Regina noticed her ability to be patient and think critically was impaired when she was sharing space with Marti. Their job is hard, sure, but this was getting ridiculous. Is it possible to be stressed out by someone else's stress?

Chemicals released in one stressed body alert the rest of the group to danger, a response that comes in handy if we all need to escape a burning building but not when it leads to collective burnout or a tense marriage. This secondhand nature of the stress reaction is one reason that stress is known as the "new smoking."

While stress is contagious, so is laughter and calm. Think about it. Aren't there some people who always make you feel better just by being around them?

Pay attention to secondhand stress symptoms and recognize:

- Other people may have different (often more negative) reactions to the same stressor. You may not find a project overwhelming, but your co-worker may.

- Other people have different needs for stress recovery. Some people need solitary time; others need to be around people. Is the person spreading stress because they're not getting what they need to disengage from stress? Are they an iguana forced into a border collie-dense environment?

- Putting the interaction in context makes a difference. Some people may just need to talk about what is causing them stress, even though it sounds like they are asking for your help. Asking, "Do you need my advice about what to do, or do you just need to vent?" can frame your reaction to the interaction and limit your emotional response to it. This is especially important in parenting teenagers!

It is okay to tell someone you are over-capacity for stress or focused on getting something done at the moment and you'd be happy to talk at a different time. They are asking for your time, energy, and attention. If it isn't an appropriate moment for you to give these things, say so.

- Noticing someone dumping their stress on you and working to change your reaction to it may short-circuit the secondhand effect. One of the things I said to myself regularly when working with a difficult co-worker was, "Dakota (not the real name) didn't wake up this morning thinking of ways to make me miserable." I could not change Dakota's negative language or how everything seemed to be a crisis, but I could change how I reacted to it. I began responding only to the substance of our communication (the task that needed to be done, for example) and not the tone. It wasn't ideal, but it decreased my psychological stress.

- A short amount of time spent with calm, encouraging people is very effective in limiting the impact of secondhand stress. Eating lunch with someone who lightens the mood is a great strategy. In a pinch, there are always funny videos to reset your stress levels. Try searching for "cats don't like things."

Strategy #3: Be proactive rather than reactive.

Sure, things can sneak up on you, but much of our psychological stress is predictable. Scheduling time throughout the day to disengage from stress and recover is more effective than trying to fit recovery in after the stress has been triggered.

Let's return to the questions at the end of the last chapter pertaining to when you might be able to fit in recovery activities. Note that you don't need to stick to the same time or activity each day. Getting ahead of psychological stress is much more effective.

Which times are you most likely to be able to fit in recovery activities:

Before work?

_____

_____

_____

_____

At midday?

_____

_____

_____

_____

As you transition from work to home?

_____

_____

_____

_____

As you transition to bedtime?

_____

_____

_____

_____

Strategy #4: Sip media, don't gulp.

While sitting in the doctor's office waiting room with her daughter, Brenda directs her attention to the television tuned to CNN. Even though she isn't really watching it, Brenda feels her stress level increasing. She feels bombarded with doom-and-gloom predictions and complicated analysis, which may or may not be of any real value or purpose. Brenda decides to move her daughter to another section of the waiting room. Reading her daughter a book is far less stressful!

According to Dr. Joanne Cantor, an expert on the psychological effects of media, there are good reasons why the daily barrage of media inputs leaves us with jangled nerves and increased stress.

Who's Who in the Book?
Learn more about Joanne Cantor, PhD on page 310.

"One area of insight into our reactions may come from recent findings in neuroscience, research that studies how the brain and body respond to the inputs it receives," Dr. Cantor explains. "For example, research on 'mirror neurons' suggests that when we watch other people engage in behavior (even when the other people are on screen), the part of our brain that plans and prepares to perform that same activity is activated."

In other words, we aren't just passively receiving all of those messages and images; our brains are figuring out how to become part of them.

Constant exposure to worrisome news increases your stress, whether or not you are actively watching or listening. Constant connection to media through our phones makes this a 24-hour-a-day phenomenon. Protect yourself from media-induced stress by:

- **Starting and ending the day quietly.** Commit to spending the first 30 minutes and the last 30 minutes you are awake without electronic interruption. Read the paper, enjoy a cup of tea or coffee (decaf if at night!), or talk with your spouse or partner. Keep the television and radio off. Turn off your cell phone, and walk past the computer without checking your e-mail or the news sites.

- **Choosing your engagement.** Staying informed is essential; however, constant exposure isn't productive. A newspaper is less anxiety-producing than a sensationalized television report or your Facebook newsfeed.

- **Choosing a different background.** Play music rather than news radio or television. Don't be afraid to ask for the channel to be changed or the program turned off in a waiting room.

- **Not mixing eating and electronics.** Try not to eat and scroll. Along with being rude to your dining companions, you are less likely to pay attention to what and how much you are eating. Your body will digest what you eat more efficiently if you eat without interruption. We all know family dinner time is vital to child development. Social interaction is also an important part of stress management. Keep the television off and relate to those around you.

- **Taking a break.** Pause for ten minutes during the day and disconnect from the computer, phone, television, and all other electronic devices. Sit back, close your eyes, and breathe deeply. Take a quick walk. Disengaging will clear your mind, allow your body and brain to quiet, and refocus your energy. If you can't make it for ten minutes without your devices, start with five minutes and build your way up to two ten-minute breaks per day.

Strategy #5: Celebrate all victories.

No matter how small, a win is a win. In our busy day, it is easy to gloss over what is completed or what is done well as we rush on to the next task. Recognizing a job well done, a mess cleaned up, a problem avoided, or an issue endured refocuses your attention on the positive.

Our brains focus on the negative in order to protect and prepare us for the things that can go bad. That negative focus can be helpful at times, but staying focused on what could go wrong or what is difficult increases psychological stress. Shifting the focus as often as you can to something positive helps relieve the stress created by the negative focus.

Stress-Proof Leadership Insight
People perform best when they feel connected to their leaders, each other, and the mission of the organization.
Read about this insight on page 263.

One great way to shift focus is to "woohoo"! A woohoo is a simple, joyous expression of something good. You can share a woohoo in person, on the phone, via e-mail, on Facebook or Twitter—wherever. By expressing something positive you shift the focus away from the negative. It doesn't have to be a big thing. It could be simply, "Woohoo! I got my taxes in on time!"

It's not bragging. It is sharing a positive part of yourself or your life with someone who really gets it. For example:

- No one understands the joy of putting away the diaper bag when the child has been potty trained better than another parent.

- Working from home, without co-workers or colleagues, it is hard to truly celebrate when something good happens. Connecting with other home-officers via e-mail definitely makes it more special.
- Sharing a "woohoo" with childhood friends on Facebook is a great way to connect with the person you were way back when.
- Shouting out to a group of like-minded people on Twitter can be very entertaining.
- Sometimes it takes someone in the same trench to truly understand and celebrate a victory.

A "woohoo" can be used to destress a crisis at work as well:

In 2007, about 5,300 kinds of pet foods were suddenly recalled from the market after some deadly contaminants were discovered in them. That year, a college friend was in charge of the customer service call center for a major manufacturer whose products included both things for people and a famous line of pet food. Before the big recall, their customer service number dedicated to the pet food rarely got a call.

Suddenly, the recall was in the news, and they were getting hundreds per day, even though nothing was wrong with their product. To cope, my friend had to train all of the personal hygiene product customer service people to handle pet food calls. And they had to know all their facts immediately.

They had one very long day to get everyone trained. Getting them up to speed on time was exhausting for everyone involved. Using one of my tips, my friend celebrated the completion of each training section with a "woohoo." They laughed about it. They even eagerly looked forward to mastering the next section. What could have been a terrible day ended up being an enjoyable team effort.

So, who or what can you woohoo?

Strategy #6: Know when enough is enough.

Sometimes the best choice is to disengage permanently from a source of stress.

Beth slows down to take the left turn toward work. With just four blocks to go, she feels her stomach tighten into an all-too-familiar knot. Taking deep breaths, Beth prepares herself for the day ahead. Maybe she'd be lucky. Shannon, the owner of the bridal shop Beth manages, doesn't come in every day. In the beginning, they got along well, and Shannon appreciated Beth's experience and expertise.

Shannon is an attorney with a busy practice who opened the store partially as an investment but mostly because she thought it would be fun. Now Shannon rarely has time for Beth unless it is to complain about how Beth handled something. The last time Shannon was in the store, she was about to put a customer in a dress that was on hold for another bride. Shannon then yelled at Beth in front of the customer when Beth pointed out the mistake. As Beth pulls into the parking lot, she sees Shannon unlocking the front door. Beth sighs. She isn't looking forward to today's complaint.

Sometimes the toll of psychological stress is insurmountable. As we discussed in the first section, evaluating the cost in time, energy, and attention in relation to the benefits is essential in maintaining a healthy stress environment. In Beth's case, the psychological toll far outweighs the benefits. Eventually, her only choice is to remove herself from the impact of Shannon's abusive behavior. On many occasions, I've asked someone who is struggling, "How long are you willing to put up with the impact of this before you say it isn't worth it? When is it enough to decide to leave?"

We each have to decide whether the benefits of an activity or job are worth the psychological toll it takes. High levels of psychological stress often manifest in physical symptoms such as:

- Indigestion
- Nausea
- Loss of appetite
- A "fight" reaction, such as a racing heart rate, shortness of breath, or feeling "on edge"
- Sleep issues
- Frequent illness
- Fatigue

Stress Detour

Did you skip to this section because your stress level is high?

You may want to skip ahead to the conclusion on page 231 and begin implementing the strategies from this section and those from the previous section. Once you've helped your body process cortisol out and you've worked to turn off the cortisol pump, return to Section 2 to learn how to reduce the stress in your environment.

Pay attention to the physical symptoms you are experiencing. These may be a clue that it is time for a change.

Of course, there are times that a stressor cannot be avoided. There might be circumstances that necessitate our staying in a job or a relationship. There are times when we are dealing with an illness or an injury—to ourselves or someone in our bubble. The next section covers what to do when there is trouble in the bubble and you have to work and live under the pressure of a situation you cannot escape.

SECTION 6

Resilience in Crisis and Change

Chapter 15

TROUBLE IN THE BUBBLE

The Problem:
Vulnerability impedes
resilience in crisis and change.

Highly capable people are often unequipped to weather the stress of an unsolvable situation.

Your bubble is the metaphorical container that holds you and the people most important to you, as we discussed on page 56. When something out of your control happens to someone in your bubble, it can create significant, and unrelenting, stress.

High-performing people are often inexperienced in accepting help and being vulnerable. For them, the stress of dealing with vulnerability amplifies the stress of crisis and change.

Stacey was in her final year of medical school when her marriage fell apart. She wished she could have ended things with Bill in a more civil manner, but the divorce was bitter and finalized just weeks before graduation. Stacey tried to make the best of it, but the achievement of graduating was tainted. Medical school had been all-consuming, and she hadn't really had a chance to deal with her feelings about the divorce. She just kept going.

A move to a new state for a residency program quickly followed graduation. Now she is working extraordinarily long hours, taking on new responsibilities, and trying to make a life in a new town where she knows no one. She feels like her world shattered, and she can't find her way. At the end of her long days, she comes home and cries. Then she beats herself up for crying. She should be able to handle all of this so much better.

Are you dealing with the curse of capability?

Capability—being the doer, the solver, the leader—can be a curse as well as a blessing. In the face of crisis and change, capable people fly into action and solve problems. When the problem isn't solvable or when we have to surrender to the idea of being helpless to fix it, change and crisis hit highly capable people the hardest.

Stress-Proof Leadership Insight
Resilient leaders are more successful.
Read about this insight on page 281.

Feeling vulnerable creates a stress reaction.

Life-threatening or life-altering events such as divorce, serious illness, and accidents leave us feeling helpless, unsafe, and weak—vulnerable. When we feel vulnerable, our natural inclination is to pull into ourselves for protection. Vulnerability makes it more challenging to engage in the world around us, connect with people who can help us, and feel good. Like Stacey, my world felt shattered after my heart attack. The knowledge that bad things can and did happen to me made the world seem too scary. Coping when your world turns upside-down takes time and effort—all injuries require time to heal.

Ultimately, resilience is a choice. We choose to move forward in the face of failure, tragedy, pain, or life-altering events we can't control. Understanding your reaction to vulnerability is essential to becoming resilient.

Resilience is a choice.

After a near-death experience, I needed to be able to summon security to move forward—to raise my girls and live my life with my husband. I coped with daily anxiety about my uncertain health by thinking through every possible situation. What would happen if I had another heart attack when I was home alone with the girls? What if I was at the grocery store? I needed to think through the steps necessary to deal with those situations. What would I need? Whom would I call?

I used the strategies to combat the uncertainty we discussed in Section 3 by digging deep into my fear and thinking through how to navigate the worst-case scenarios. While this allowed me to feel confident enough to leave the house, challenge myself to exercise, and travel for work, I was still having trouble coping with feeling vulnerable.

Emotional responses to vulnerability can be confusing.

The vulnerability caused by change and crisis creates a potent cocktail of emotional responses that can continue to trigger the cortisol stress response. Like Stacey, I felt I should be able to handle it better and worried that my emotional reactions were inappropriate.

I felt both euphoric at having survived my heart attack and angry at the loss of the type of birth we had planned for our daughters. So many people told me how lucky I was, but I didn't always feel blessed. I laughed at bad news. The smallest things seemed to make me angry. I cried in the shower a lot.

But yet, it was also one of the most joyous times of our lives. Experiencing joy and pain at the same time can be confusing and uncomfortable. My anger seemed out of place in the midst of the joy of our new family, and it reminded me of the mix of pain and joy when my father passed away. In the midst of grieving, I reconnected and laughed with family and friends and celebrated professional accomplishments.

One of the most challenging things to navigate is feeling joy in the midst of grief or pain, particularly when someone we love is sick or has passed away. Sometimes we think we don't deserve happiness or feel like we are dishonoring the person by not being sad all of the time. We are complicated creatures capable of feeling more than one thing at a time.

What I came to understand was that life-altering events trigger a mix of responses that often feel out of control or just plain wrong. That's okay. Recognizing that those emotions are a response to vulnerability and giving myself space to heal was vital. Just like Stacey, I needed to be kind to myself, accept my reactions as normal, and then work through them.

There are good days and bad days. It is okay to feel the way you do; you are experiencing a normal emotional reaction. Saying, "I shouldn't feel like this" doesn't allow you to process what you are feeling. Giving yourself space to sort through your emotions and seeking help if that seems too difficult is the sort of kindness we would extend to others in the same situation.

Self-kindness is often the key to resilience in the face of unrelenting stress in crisis and change. The next chapter offers strategies to become more resilient.

Chapter 16

PRACTICING RESILIENCE

Stress-Proof Skill

Get comfortable with vulnerability to become resilient in crisis and change.

For the times when all of the other strategies in this book are not quite enough, I offer these eight lessons to get comfortable with feeling vulnerable:

1. Get comfortable with anger.
2. Accept help.
3. Give yourself a break.
4. Focus on what is possible rather than dwelling on what is difficult.
5. Notice the good stuff.
6. Embrace a sense of humor.
7. Let go.
8. Don't go it alone.

Lesson #1: Get comfortable with anger.

Change and crisis usually come with a side order of loss.

Even when a change is predominantly good, there is an element of loss—of what is familiar—which can create anger. When the change is unwelcome and out of our control, the loss can be significant. Sadness over the loss makes us feel even more vulnerable, so in some ways, anger is easier.

Anger triggers a chemical reaction in the body, too. Instead of cortisol, adrenaline floods the system, which raises our heart rate and can help us get fired up to take action. As we discussed in Section 4, increasing your heart rate and letting it come back down again can reduce your cortisol level. In the end, getting angry could reduce your stress. But that, of course, depends on how well you can release that anger. If you stay mad, your heart rate and cortisol levels remain elevated.

Anger can be a potent motivator in recovery. For example, Ken was the doer in all of his relationships.

Ken's friends and family knew he could be counted on in any situation, especially in a crisis. He was quick to jump in and took pride in being able to solve a problem or ease a struggle. So why was he so angry now that he needs help? A car accident crushed his sternum and damaged both of his knees. Everything hurts, and he can't do the simplest of tasks for himself. He couldn't even go back to his own apartment after he left the hospital. Now friends and family have gathered to take turns helping out, but nothing seems right. He hates appearing weak and allowing people to see him so out of sorts.

"*Damn it! You said I'd be done with this stupid thing,*" bellowed Ken. *He was tired of having to move the little balls in the device that measured how deeply he was breathing. It hurt to take deep breaths, and he was frustrated that his recovery was going slower than he'd hoped.*

"*I know, Ken,*" *said Sal, the visiting nurse,* "*but we can't risk you getting pneumonia.*"

Ken felt terrible; he knew Sal was on his side. "*I'm sorry, I just don't know why I am so angry all the time.*"

"*It makes perfect sense to me,*" *said Sal.* "*You're trapped in a situation where you have very little control. Anger is a perfect response to feeling vulnerable.*"

"*It doesn't feel perfect,*" *scoffed Ken.*

"*It may feel uncomfortable, sure, but we all have the instinct to protect ourselves—and sometimes that comes out as anger. Please don't feel bad about it. I have patients yell at me all the time,*" *Sal said with a wink.* "*Those are the ones I know are going to be okay. I mean, don't be a total jerk about it, but if you are getting angry, it means you are up for a fight. Let's put that to work to get you better!*"

Sal is right.

Our natural reaction to feeling vulnerable is often anger.

It makes sense that anger is one of the stages of grief. When we are already feeling vulnerable, it doesn't take much to tip us into anger. After my heart attack, I would get angry at the smallest things—having to struggle to put on the stupid support stockings, for example.

It wasn't really about the socks; I just hated to be reminded of my uncertain health, and it hurt my chest incision to bend over to put them on. I remember throwing a rolled-up stocking across the room and yelling some salty words one day.

I learned to get comfortable with that anger and ask myself what was making me feel vulnerable. In that case, the incision on my leg, where my surgeon harvested the vein to fix my heart, wasn't healing well. I had an infection, which was hopefully clearing up, but it was still gross and needed daily attention. Of course, that made me feel vulnerable and angry.

After the burst of anger passed, I actually felt better. Letting it out helped. I've never been particularly comfortable with anger— both feeling it and being on the receiving end. I needed to learn to get comfortable with letting myself feel anger and then letting it subside. I did my best to direct my anger at things rather than people.

Some anger can be healthy, but too much can be a problem. If you are feeling angry most of the time, it is probably time to talk with someone. Needing help was one of my biggest anger triggers, which leads me to the next lesson.

Lesson #2: Accept help.

It's okay to need help. It's also okay not to like that you need it.

By definition, needing help makes you feel vulnerable, so our reactions to receiving help can be confusing. Mine certainly were after the girls were born.

We were so lucky to be surrounded by people who wanted to help, though I often had a hard time accepting it. Our freezer was full of food, and people came into our home to help with chores and with the girls. I felt like I SHOULD be able to do things for myself and didn't like having to rely on other people. I am pretty opinionated about HOW things should be done, and I don't think I'm alone in this, among other highly capable people.

When I went into the hospital with preterm labor, we were in the midst of a kitchen and powder room remodel. We didn't have a dishwasher, and with the girls on the way, it was time to change that. Of course, as home improvement projects usually go, that small change led to a new counter, new floor, new sinks, new toilet...you get the picture. The contents of our kitchen were in boxes in the dining room.

Should I have been thrilled that our family and neighbors came in and finished the job, including putting all of the contents of the drawers and cupboards away before I arrived home? Probably. My reaction was to sit down at the kitchen table and cry. Nothing was where I would have put it. I'd missed out on finishing the project. I wasn't sure if I was sad or mad; it was confusing. It didn't take too long for me to realize that what was most important was the caring expressed by the gift of their time, not the way it was delivered.

An episode of Oprah featuring Dr. Phil I'd watched in the hospital turned out to be essential learning for me. Dr. Phil was working with a couple with small children. The wife was overwhelmed and complaining that her husband wasn't helping with the kids. Roll the video footage...and soon we see her criticizing every little thing he tried to do. No wonder he stopped trying!

I so could have been that wife! Even now, especially on the boat, I like certain things to be done the right way—my way, of course!

Here is what Dr. Phil said: "You can have help, or you can have it done your way. Not both. Which do you want most?"

Hmmm...good question.

To this day, I find myself saying that phrase to myself fairly often. *What do I really want? Help or my way?* It depends on the situation.

Here's the key: once you choose (help or your way), you can't complain. If you accept help, it isn't fair to complain about how that help is given. If you want it your way, don't complain about doing all the work.

Once I opened myself up to receiving help and reminded myself to accept it as it was given, I was able to use that help to get through the tough times.

The other thing to remember about accepting help is that it can feel like a gift to the giver. If you are usually the doer, the giver, the highly capable person in the relationship, the other person may not have very many opportunities to give to you. Being able to help you "evens things up" in the relationship and resets the dynamic in ways that can be very welcome.

Lesson #3: Give yourself a break.

Giving yourself permission to step away from the stress of caring for a loved one, your own illness, relationship issues, or financial issues is essential to being able to withstand the challenge.

If a job needed to be done, people gave it to Sara. She always prided herself on her ability to handle any situation, no matter how challenging. Sara fought her way through a male-dominated industry and gained the trust and respect of frontline workers. She took all projects head-on and found difficult situations exhilarating.

Her superiors always knew she could be counted on to bring in a project on time and on budget. Her co-workers relied on her excellent judgment and support. Her friends knew she was the most capable of their group. She and her husband were partners in the best sense. They raised a family and established a standing in the community.

Through it all, Sara kept a close focus on keeping herself and her family healthy, well connected, and content. There was always a way to make it through a tough time to see the light at the end of the tunnel. She handled it all until the day her husband was diagnosed with late-stage lung cancer. Weeks later, her job was eliminated due to a merger. Suddenly, nothing made sense. A lifetime runner, she knew this feeling: she had nothing left. She had hit a wall. For the first time in her life, she couldn't fix it.

Caring for someone you love through an illness is complicated. I've been both the person who needs care and a caretaker for someone I love dearly. I'd rather be sick. Being the caretaker is not only emotionally and physically draining, but it also carries significant guilt about taking time to care for yourself.

For Sara, her daily run became an escape from the things she couldn't control. She initially felt guilty about taking the time to exercise, but if she didn't run, the stress built up. She had to get over the guilt of caring for herself and recognize that care was what made it possible for her to deal with everything else. She needed to get out of caretaker mode and just be Sara for a while.

When we were caring for my father-in-law after he was diagnosed with pancreatic cancer while also raising our then-five-year-old girls, our life was full of challenges. I felt terrible and selfish about taking time to exercise, nap, or just do something I enjoyed. But disconnecting from the ongoing crisis was the thing that kept me sane. I needed to disengage from everything going on at home and recharge.

Whether you are caring for a loved one or raising children, taking time to care for yourself is essential.

Here are some ways to take a break:

- Watch a dumb sitcom to make you laugh
- Chat with a friend on the phone
- Get out:

  ❯ Go to a museum
  ❯ Go to a movie
  ❯ Take a walk or run outside
  ❯ Have coffee or an adult beverage with a good friend

- Practice retail therapy (within reason)

- Volunteer in a rewarding way
- Exercise
- Take a trip
- Make music

Whether you are caring for someone you love, dealing with your own illness, experiencing relationship issues, or facing financial woes, it can be hard in the midst of an ongoing crisis to take a break. It can feel selfish, but it isn't. The strategies for recovering from stress detailed in Section 2 are very helpful, as is giving yourself permission to take a break and use them. Find resources for caregivers at StressProofResources.com.

Lesson #4: Focus on what is possible rather than dwelling on what is difficult.

Some people face an excruciatingly difficult time in their lives (illness, the untimely death of a loved one, or losing a job, for example) and can rally themselves and go forward, while others get stuck and never seem to move on. The difference has everything to do with the former group's ability to identify the possibilities and focus on that.

Sometimes it is just a simple task done well. Other times it is the smile of a friend's face when you greet her, the pride in someone asking for your opinion, or closing the book on a project well done. Some days you have to look a little harder to find things that are possible to achieve. Even on the worst days, they are there.

The first few days after my heart attack, I felt very disconnected from reality, and things felt out of control. I kept thinking to myself, "This is not how it is supposed to be!"

I had all sorts of expectations about what the first few days with my new family would be like:

- Witnessing the miracle of birth
- Marveling over healthy babies
- Holding them right after birth and singing "Happy Birthday"
- Enjoying quiet moments with just our new family
- Making excited phone calls to family and friends

While going through a significant crisis, we often dwell on what is difficult and what didn't meet our expectations. Focusing on the negative is easy to do when everything seems to be wrong. After my heart attack, I remembered something that my father used in his practice as a psychologist. The concept of "awfulizing"—he made up the word—describes what happens when the rug is pulled out from underneath you and you are drawn into a cycle of thinking everything is terrible:

- The entire situation sucks.
- It's not getting better.
- It likely will never get better.
- There isn't a way out.
- And, well, it's just awful.

"Quit your awfulizing!" he would say. When you are caught in the downward spiral of awfulizing, it is hard not to feel out of control. The way out of the spiral is to find something you CAN control.

Another of my expectations was to breastfeed the girls. During my pregnancy, I had attended classes and researched nursing twins.

Exclusively breastfeeding twins would be a challenge, but I was determined to try. After open-heart surgery and with the girls born prematurely, was breastfeeding possible? No one was sure, but I was willing to try and would be happy with whatever was possible. At first, the girls were not ready to nurse at all, and I was recovering from having my sternum cut open, among other things. Not too many patients in the intensive care unit have a lactation specialist visit them, but we made the best of it. It wasn't easy—the girls had to learn to suck and swallow, and I had to learn how to make it work. But eventually, we all got the hang of it. Doing this simple thing for them made me feel like I could do something "normal." It was something I could control, and it was a gift.

Focusing on my breastfeeding victory was key to withstanding the rest of the uncertainty I was facing at the time.

Lesson #5: Notice the good stuff.

In the midst of unrelenting stress, it is easy to lose sight of what is good in your life. Much like focusing on what is possible, noticing the uplifting things is essential. One practice I find helpful is writing down three good things at the end of each day. There have been days where coming up with three things was tough. One day I wrote "I'm a very safe driver." The practice of looking for uplifting parts of your life refocuses your thoughts and can improve your mood and ability to deal with challenges. We can often feel guilty about enjoying life in the midst of difficult times. That joy, however, can be the key to resilience.

Here are some other suggestions for uplifting your spirits:

- Keep a journal of gratitude

- Do things that make you happy, even if you don't feel like it (another example of behaving your way to success)
- Smile or sing
- Make a playlist of uplifting and energizing songs
- Make an album of uplifting photos to flip through on your phone
- Google "Aussies doing things"

Lesson #6: Embrace a sense of humor.

When you are in over your head, it is good to be able to laugh about it.

When the girls were about nine months old, I was asked to throw out the first pitch at a major league baseball game. Even with all my dance training, I have never been particularly sporty and really had no business being around any sport involving throwing or catching a ball. Clay tried, early in our relationship, to teach me to play softball, but after the ball rolled out of my glove, down my arm, and smashed my sunglasses, he finally understood the problem. My contribution to the softball league was keeping score—at which I am quite good. Nevertheless, how many people get to throw the first pitch? It sounded like fun.

Clay thought I was nuts. He was sure that I would throw the ball into the dirt and people would boo me. "They booed the president; why wouldn't they boo you?" he exclaimed. I decided I didn't care. It was worth the risk to have such a unique experience.

Clay, good sport that he is, bought me a baseball for Mother's Day and started coaching me. We measured off the distance across the front yards on our street, and he (and the neighbors) gave me pitching lessons and encouragement. I practiced and was able to throw a decent ball. Right up to the moment I walked out on the field, Clay was incredibly supportive. He kept telling me, "Block out everything else. Just focus on the catcher. Keep looking at the catcher, and you'll do just fine. You can do this." We talked about where to stand, and I was ready. After shaking hands with the catcher, I prepared to walk out onto the field.

As we started onto the field, the catcher turned to me and said, "Good luck. I'm not wearing a cup. Don't hurt me!" and then ran off for home plate. Chuckling, I walked to the pitcher's mound. As I turned and he nodded that we were ready, I laughed harder. As I tried to focus, he squatted and assumed the catcher position—I couldn't really look at him. His words kept echoing in my head: "I'm not wearing a cup...I'm not wearing a cup."

It was time, and I threw the ball. I'm not sure exactly what happened, but the ball went kind of sideways and ended up bouncing and rolling to the first baseline. On the giant screen, my name and "survived a heart attack while pregnant with twins" flashed up. So rather than boos, I heard thousands of people go "Aww..." My husband says they all thought I'd sustained some sort of disability from my heart attack. Rather than being embarrassed, I found the whole thing hilarious. I know I haven't always had a sense of humor about myself, but I've found it essential when embracing new challenges.

When I got pregnant and knew there was a possibility we'd have twins, some of my friends started teasing me immediately about how big I would get. They made jokes about having to use a boatlift to get me aboard a sailboat or rolling me up the stairs. As I got larger and larger, I became more and more of a klutz. Even my mom began to joke that I should have an alarm like trucks have when they back up. I learned quickly to laugh at myself, and it turned out to be an essential lesson for the time ahead. Our family has a saying: "If you can laugh about it, it can't be that bad." It's true.

These are lighthearted examples of a more significant point: having a sense of humor, not taking things too seriously when they don't work out exactly as planned, is essential.

We all make mistakes, but the biggest mistake is never trying! The most significant risk is not taking one!

Embrace a sense of humor, and risk being wrong or looking foolish. Things may not work out exactly as you planned. What do you wish you could do but are worried about trying? Try anyway. Without risk, there is no zest!

Lesson #7: Let go.

What are you rehashing?

Conflicts with other people often create lingering stress. We rehash conversations and confrontations in our minds and drum up psychological stress. Let's revisit Beth's story from Chapter 14:

Beth left her job managing the bridal shop at the end of her three-year contract and gave the owner, Shannon, two months to hire a new manager. Beth even trained the new manager so that the transition would be seamless. Things spiraled downward as Beth completed her final days. According to her contract, Beth was due a bonus based on sales during the final quarter of her employment. Shannon, angered by Beth's abandonment, refused to pay it. Shannon, a lawyer, drew up the contract and claimed Beth breached the agreement by leaving two days before the end of the quarter.

Beth filed a complaint in small claims court, and at the hearing Shannon didn't show up, sending a partner from her law firm instead. The partner presented a statement from Shannon claiming Beth stole items from the shop. Beth was enraged by the accusation but followed the advice of her lawyer and kept her mouth shut. Her lawyer defended Beth, and Shannon's lawyer quickly retracted the statement.

While the judge decided in Beth's favor, she was still outraged at being called a thief. Months after the hearing, Beth couldn't let go of her anger. Mulling over thoughts of why Shannon chose to be so mean kept her awake at night. Finally a friend asked why she was hanging on to something she couldn't change. Beth thought about it.

Shannon's behavior after Beth left wasn't completely out of character. Beth witnessed Shannon demoralizing vendors in a power play to gain better pricing. Shannon talked about former friends who displeased her in some way as enemies to be punished. Beth realized this behavior wasn't directed at her individually. Shannon's reaction to challenge was to strike out. Beth's friend offered a phrase to keep in mind: "What if this is the best Shannon can do?" Any time Beth started to think about how Shannon had treated her, she remembered the phrase. If this was really the best Shannon could do, Beth had to let go of her bad feelings about it. The best Beth can do is to move forward, remembering to be kind to herself and not let other people's behavior impact her vitality.

What do you need to let go?

Over the years, three questions have been very helpful to my clients (and to me) in the process of letting go:

1. What if this is the best they can do?

In Beth's case, she would ask herself, "What if this is the best Shannon can do?" Asking this question allows Beth to take herself out of the equation and look at it from a different perspective. Perhaps Shannon is constantly on the defensive because of something in her past or because of challenges Beth doesn't understand. Maybe Shannon's way of creating a predictable life is always to strike first. Ultimately, Shannon's behavior isn't directed at Beth. Beth is in the path of Shannon's behavior. A tornado isn't concerned about what is in its path; neither is Shannon.

2. What is more important—being right or feeling better?

We all want to be treated fairly and have our work valued. When we are wronged, it is often hard to let go because we don't get our moment of closure. Without an apology or even the opportunity to express our feelings about the situation, it is difficult to let go.

3. What will alleviate these bad feelings?

Sometimes we need to create that closure for ourselves. Writing a letter to the person who wronged you and then burning it, for example, can be cathartic. Choosing to prioritize our own happiness, momentum, as well as our physical and emotional health is a victory to be celebrated. How will you celebrate letting go?

Lesson #8: Don't go it alone.

You'd seek help if you cut yourself deeply. Trouble in your bubble is a wound, too—but you don't see the blood. It's okay to seek advice from a professional to help you or to find someone who has experienced something similar.

Stress-Proof Leadership Insight
Effective leaders have courageous small conversations.
Read about this insight on page 278.

It would be best if you also asked for what you need. Early in my recovery, sleep did not come easily because of the fear that I wouldn't wake up again. I needed someone to be in the room with me while I slept. Even though it seemed childish, I asked my mom to sit with me while I napped. That's what I needed.

Building a circle of support when going through change or crisis is crucial. In my experience, you may be surprised at whom you can rely on in challenging times. Good friends may not be equipped to support you, while acquaintances may step up and become lifelines. You may also need to get professional help to weather the physical, emotional, and spiritual challenges.

Many people dealing with crisis shut down emotionally. They stop feeling anything. This, from the outside, may seem like capability in action. On the contrary, it may be a sign that the person has pulled so far into themselves that they aren't even noticing they need help. As I often say, I don't have letters after my name, and you shouldn't confuse my lessons with medical advice. But if you or someone in your life are experiencing signs like the ones listed below (which, again, are not intended to diagnose or treat mental illness), I encourage you to consult your doctor or a trained psychologist or psychiatrist:

- People noticing your poor performance at work
- Deteriorating relationships (having difficulty understanding others)
- Withdrawing from friends or family
- Confused thoughts
- Changes in sex drive
- Daily use of alcohol or other substances to deal with stress
- Having trouble completing daily living tasks such as bathing or feeding yourself

- Not sleeping three or more nights per week for several weeks
- Thoughts of "giving up" or harming yourself
- Thoughts or plans of suicide or hurting others

Seeking professional help is not a sign of weakness, but the stigma of mental illness and the complexities of the mental health system often create barriers, which makes getting help harder.

Most of us don't talk about seeing a therapist with our friends and family, but we probably should. Talking about mental health normalizes it and makes getting help easier for others. If we would talk about it, we'd discover that many of us have sought professional help at some point to deal with grief, relationship issues, stress, clinical conditions, or dependency.

I know how overwhelming it can be to navigate systems to find the services we need. For me, the mental health providers within our insurance plan were listed on an entirely separate website than the physical health providers—an almost invisible website. The only way I found the mental health website was to call the insurance company. Asking for help is already a vulnerable action; it really shouldn't be that hard to get to the appropriate services.

I compiled a list of up-to-date mental health resources, which you can find at StressProofResources.com.

One of my favorite resources is the National Alliance on Mental Illness (NAMI). Their website, NAMI.org, has a wealth of information, and they provide peer-support services, resources, and referrals by telephone—1-800-950-NAMI (6264)—or e-mail—info@nami.org. NAMI also offers an extensive online library of valuable information and answers to frequently asked questions.

NAMI provides a helpline, not a hotline, crisis line, or suicide prevention line. If your stress has gotten to the point that you're thinking of hurting yourself or someone else, go to the nearest emergency room or call 911 immediately.

- You can also call the **National Suicide Prevention Lifeline** at **800-273-TALK (8255)**. You don't even need to give your name to talk with a trained crisis counselor (available 24 hours every day). The National Suicide Prevention Lifeline connects with local crisis centers in the Lifeline network.

- Text **NAMI** to **741-741** to connect with a trained crisis counselor to receive free, 24/7 crisis support via text message.

- Call **800-799-SAFE (7233)** to reach the **National Domestic Violence Hotline** with trained expert advocates available 24/7 to provide confidential support to anyone experiencing domestic violence or seeking resources and information. Help is available in Spanish and other languages.

- Call **800-656-HOPE (4673)** to connect with a trained **National Sexual Assault Hotline** staff member from a sexual assault service provider in your area offering access to a range of free services 24/7.

Weathering the storm.

Self-kindness is one of the most impactful gifts when you are in the midst of crisis and change. To support resilience and get comfortable with vulnerability, remember to:

- Be gentle as you judge your reactions.
- Build a circle of support.
- Seek the help you need.
- Give yourself permission to implement the strategies in this book to help you process and recover from stress so that you can find vitality even in the face of distress.

Conclusion

PRACTICING A
STRESS-PROOF LIFESTYLE

The tools in this book aren't abstract ideas for me—they're literally life-or-death skills. In the years since my heart attack, I've lived with fear and uncertainty, but these tools allow me to get up every day, work, and enjoy my family. I was lucky; most women don't survive their first heart attack.

My surgeon repaired my heart, though a small part of it doesn't beat anymore. Even though my pregnancy caused the heart attack, I am at high risk of having another, and controlling my risk factors is essential. I can control my diet and be physically active, but stress is an exponential multiplier of risk that I simply can't afford.

For nearly two decades, I've used my own risk to motivate me to offer better solutions for others. After a heart attack, the cesarean section delivery of the girls, and open-heart surgery, I woke up in the ICU knowing I'd been given my life story for a reason. It has been my honor to use it as a national spokesperson for the American Heart Association, to lobby Congress on behalf of the HEART for Women Act, and most recently to serve as a paid spokesperson for the Take Cholesterol to Heart campaign. However, I know that merely having information rarely changes behavior.

Real change becomes possible only when we connect information to something we hold dear. What keeps me up at night is the thought of not being here for my family's important moments. I was given the gift of a heart attack at age 35 and know that if I want to see my girls graduate from college, I have to protect my heart from stress.

Information doesn't change behavior.

You would think that surviving a heart attack at age 35 while pregnant with twins would be enough to turn me into a workout-crazed fitness queen.

It wasn't.

I had lots of information. The doctors told me a full recovery depended on exercising 30 minutes every day, but I wasn't doing it. The information wasn't enough to change my behavior.

When the girls were about six months old, my husband, Clay, put things in perspective. He was concerned about my rather lackluster efforts at exercise and told me I needed to do better. He was right, but I wasn't motivated. Too many other things needed my attention (and frankly, I just didn't feel like exercising). Honestly, the last thing I wanted to do at the end of the day was get on the stupid stationary bike in the family room for 30 minutes.

He was having none of it. Looking me in the eye one day, he said, "Honey, nothing else you do makes any difference to the girls and me unless you are here. You are our whole world. You need to do the work to be sure you are still around."

That certainly brought clarity. If I didn't take care of myself, how could I take care of the people I loved? If I didn't take care of myself, how would I be part of their future? We struggled through years of infertility treatments to get these girls; I wasn't about to miss out on seeing them grow up.

In that moment, I got it. It's not about the number on the scale or the size of a pair of pants. It's about maintaining a body healthy enough to get you where you want to go. The price of admission to the future I want with my husband, daughters, and future grandchildren is moving around 30 minutes every day, managing my risk factors, and controlling my stress. It is a small price I'm happy to pay—as long as I remember why I'm doing it.

That is the essence of a stress-proof life, protecting your vitality, and getting to all the moments you don't want to miss.

Stress isn't good or bad; it is a natural reaction to your environment. The skills in this book provide a system to deal strategically with the cortisol reaction so that you can live and work well under pressure and protect your bubble of contentment.

Reading this book is a good first step. The next step is committing to doing something different.

One of the ways I serve my audiences and readers best is to illustrate the connection between the information about their health (what we need to do) and the motivation for protecting it (why we do it). We all have moments in life we don't want to miss. For me, there are many: crying a little when we leave our daughters at college, seeing them fall in love, dancing with my wonderful husband at their weddings, and welcoming their children into our family. I can't rely on luck; I have to do the work to get there. We all do. I'm proud to provide the tools and motivation so that my readers get to have all their moments too.

The following process walks you through how to create a plan to implement the stress-proof skills. I've spent nearly two decades asking people to change their behavior, and I have a few techniques to do it:

1. Don't try to change everything right now.
2. Create a small, specific, and achievable daily habit.
3. Connect what you want with what you need to do.
4. Reward yourself.
5. Don't get caught up in perfection.

Technique #1: Don't try to change everything right now.

It may seem like you need to change everything right now. You don't. In fact, committing to big sweeping changes in behavior rarely works because they are too hard to sustain. Let's focus on something you CAN do for a specific period of time.

Technique #2: Create a small, specific, and achievable daily habit.

A daily habit is another example of behaving your way to success. If you can do something small every day for 100 days, you have changed your default behavior. That small change can make a big difference in your ability to live and work well under pressure. What can you do every day for the next 100 days to begin stress-proofing? Here are some examples:

- Singing while you drive to work
- Taking the dog for a walk
- Going to bed the same day you woke up.

- Setting an alarm to remind yourself to disconnect from the source of psychological stress
- Starting each day by removing any task that does not support your bubble
- Making a list at the end of the day that reminds you of the intangible benefits of your work
- Celebrating a victory every day
- Setting an alarm to stand up every hour and repeat something to yourself, such as: "I will not allow things I cannot control to impact my vitality."
- Doing the right behavior for 15 minutes (starting the project you dread, paying bills, writing, etc.)

What is one small thing you can do every day for 90 days? The more specific you can be, the better.

Technique #3: Connect what you want with what you need to do.

How do you find the motivation to perform your new habit every day? The risk of disease sometime in the future isn't very motivating. Truth be told, we are far more motivated by what we value than by what we fear. Denial takes over, and you can easily push away warnings of illness or death. Connecting your health with being able to share in the things you value will make the difference.

The stress-proof skills will get you to the moments you don't want to miss. How can you focus on those moments to keep yourself motivated to do the stress-proofing work?

Creating an "I will because" statement connects the strategies you have identified to process the cortisol out of your system and protect your heart with the motivation of the moments you are unwilling to miss.

We all find our motivation in different moments. Choosing one small daily habit for 90 days and connecting it to a specific moment you don't want to miss is the key to successful stress-proofing.

What moment are you unwilling to miss?

- Is there a graduation, wedding, birth, anniversary, or other event you don't want to miss?
- Do you imagine spending your retirement on the golf course, on a sailboat, or in your garden?
- Do you long to see the Great Wall or some other exotic place?
- Is there something you've always wanted to try or experience?

My moment:

_____

Write your "I will because" statement:

I will

_____

Because I want

_____

Technique #4: Reward yourself.

Here's another thing I discovered: Rewards are very motivating! Clay again is responsible for this realization. He challenged me to exercise for at least 20 minutes every day for 100 days and offered to buy me anything I wanted if I could meet the challenge. (He knew, of course, that I would never ask for anything too extravagant!)

Exercising every day for 100 days seemed impossible, but the promise of a reward made me start. Then something interesting happened. In an odd combination of pride, habit, and desire for a reward, it became easier to get started each day. I amazingly wanted to work out. I started feeling better, and my body wanted to move.

The trick is to figure out what rewards, big and small, will encourage you to keep going. The "carrot" Clay offered got me started, but what kept me going was a daily reward of a small bowl of low-fat chocolate ice cream. I love ice cream, and I don't often allow myself to indulge in it, so that scoop was heaven. My internal dialogue about "I don't want to get on the stupid bike" was drowned out by "I WANT ICE CREAM!"

You may find it helpful to create a "carrot" for yourself each day. In addition, celebrating by the week and month can keep you motivated as well. Over the years, I've given myself many different types of rewards, from a new treadmill to a spa day.

Some days are harder than others, of course. I've missed days along the way. In fact, on my first try I built up 80 days and then got the stomach flu. However, missing one day didn't derail me; I started again and made it. Over the years, I've built up hundreds of days. Clay has built up thousands, and yes, he's missed a few as well. But it is a habit that works well, and it has worked for many other people, too.

Keeping your daily commitment deserves celebration and reward. As you build up days, schedule times to reward your commitment to yourself, not only celebrating the one hundredth day, but the first, fifth, and twenty-fifth as well.

Find a carrot to get you to put your shoes on, get off the chair, and get moving—or to do whatever other actions you need to take to protect your health and wellness. Completing the 100-Day Challenge is a huge accomplishment, and it deserves a special reward.

What reward will you give yourself for performing your task each day?

How will you celebrate the milestones of 25, 50, and 100 days?

Technique #5: Don't get caught up in perfection.

Building a new habit can be challenging. There may be a time when you step off the path you've charted. That's okay. Get back on the path. Beating yourself up for your lack of perfection doesn't move you forward. Reassess, recommit to your small change, and keep going.

How will you remind yourself to keep going?

> "Life is not about perfection.
> It's about moving in the right direction."

My goal with this book is to provide tools to help you along your own path. Know that I'm working and stumbling along my path to maintaining a stress-proof life right along with you.

Come share your journey and "I will because" statements at IWillBecause.com or on social media with the hashtag #IWillBecause. You can find more tips and articles and ask questions on my blog: EmbraceYourHeart.com.

May your stress-proof life carry you to all of the moments you look forward to experiencing. I wish you a lifetime of low stress and great success!

EXECUTIVE SUMMARY

Dear busy reader,

A book on stress shouldn't cause stress! The following is a "quick and dirty" version of this book. You can use it in a few ways:

- If you need to be familiar enough with the concepts to have a conversation with someone who encouraged you to read this book (or assigned it to you), review this summary and you should be set.
- If you want to cherry-pick the strategies, read the summary and flip to the pages that interest you.
- If you need a quick review after reading the book, the summary is an easy way to find what you need.

The Big Concept: Stress-Proof

The stress-proofing method pulls from my research on job stress and nearly two decades of working with and interviewing high performers who operate within environments of unrelenting stress. I developed the system with input from emergency room nurses, construction firms, NASA, large corporations, start-up companies, manufacturing firms, and others—probably, someone facing stressors just like yours. Stress-proofing your life means that you can perform and live an enjoyable life in the face of stress you cannot avoid.

Stress is a natural part of life, but too much stress drags down productivity and impedes our enjoyment of work and life. Rather than providing a zing of energy needed to complete a task or deal with a challenge, the physical reaction to unrelenting stress threatens health and decreases our ability to think clearly and creatively.

Stress-proofing combines skills to limit the physical impact of cortisol, promote stress recovery, and deal with the challenges of overwhelm and uncertainty.

Much like a flu shot can prevent or lessen the impact of influenza, becoming stress-proof means building immunity to stressors you cannot avoid. Stress-proofing protects health and performance against stress.

Over years working with high performers, interviewing leaders and employees, and researching job stress, I identified six problems created by high levels of stress and the skills to solve them.

Problem	Stress-Proof Skill
High stress destroys the capacity for a purposeful and enjoyable life.	Treat stress management as a HARD skill.
Overwhelm intensifies stress.	Overcome overwhelm by intentionally reordering your stress environment
Uncertainty crowds out rational thought.	Combat uncertainty by manufacturing security.
High stress causes physical damage.	Offset the physical impact of stress by effectively processing cortisol.
Psychological stress keeps cortisol flowing.	Recover from psychological stress by disconnecting from the source.
Vulnerability impedes resilience in crisis and change.	Get comfortable with vulnerability to become resilient in crisis and change.

I wrote *Stress-Proof Your Life* as a guide for people who are dealing with unrelenting stress caused by overwhelm and uncertainty. The following pages summarize each of the problems and skills. You may also want to read the Leadership Insights beginning on page 257.

Section 1 is an overview of the process of stress-proofing.

Problem #1	Stress-Proof Skill
High stress destroys the capacity for a purposeful and enjoyable life.	Treat stress management as a HARD skill.

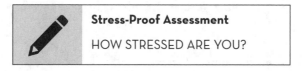

Stress-Proof Assessment
HOW STRESSED ARE YOU?

Solving the problem of unrelenting stress.

The physical and psychological impact of unrelenting stress threatens your health, decreases productivity, and blocks the ability to react rationally and creatively. With diverse symptoms such as irritability, stomach upset, and sleeplessness, stress is often challenging to quantify.

I developed a Stress Level Index as part of my research on job stress. The result of this index indicates how likely it is that your stress will impact your physical health, quality of life, and performance.

We can't alleviate all stress, and we wouldn't want to even if we could. Some stress is natural and necessary; it is what gives us the zing of energy to get things done. The zing is the result of the hormone cortisol flooding the system when the body detects danger or stress. Cortisol quickens reactions, increases pulse and blood pressure, and even thickens the blood (to prevent bleeding to death in case of injury).

Trouble comes when that zing becomes a constant thrum, continually triggering the cortisol response rather than allowing it to ebb and flow as we need it. Thicker blood, higher blood pressure, and increased pulse all make the heart work harder, which is why prolonged high stress doubles the risk of heart attack and stroke.

Rather than addressing the symptoms of stress, stress-proofing uses assessments, strategies, and tools designed to help you manage your stress environment and put simple practices into place to protect yourself from unavoidable stress and support your quality of life and performance. The next sections detail how to use the stress-proofing skills to:

- address the source of stress
- protect your physical health and emotional well-being
- safeguard your productivity
- enhance your quality of life

Section 2 details how to overcome overwhelm.

▮▮▮ Problem #2	👤 Stress-Proof Skill
Overwhelm intensifies stress.	Overcome overwhelm by intentionally reordering your stress environment

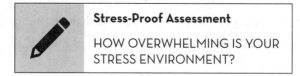

Stress-Proof Assessment

HOW OVERWHELMING IS YOUR STRESS ENVIRONMENT?

Overwhelm creates a crisis of urgency.

In our busy lives, we rarely stop to examine the swirl of demands for our time, energy, and attention. Overwhelm makes us feel like we can't keep up. If everything is urgently important, nothing can be a priority. What often is blamed on lack of organization or poor time management usually turns out to be overwhelm-induced confusion of urgency. This problem is discussed in Chapter 3 beginning on page 31.

We live in an environment of stress.

An environment is the collection of things, people, conditions, and forces that surround us. A stress environment is made up of the swirl of things, activities, obligations, people, conditions, and forces calling for our time, energy, and attention.

Ecology is the process of examining and tending to the relationships and interaction of things in our environment. Stress ecology is the process of intentionally reordering the expenditure of time, energy, and attention on the items swirling around us.

Stress-proofing uses these concepts to stifle the cry of things, people, and obligations calling for our time, energy, and attention; promote satisfaction and productivity; and insulate us from unrelenting stress.

The first step of taming overwhelm is getting a clear look at the items in your personal stress environment and how much they add to or detract from your vitality. Chapter 4, beginning on page 37, details a process to:

- Identify what is calling for your time, energy, and attention.
- Determine the organization of your stress environment.
- Evaluate the relative value of the items in terms of how they support your vitality (your capacity for a purposeful and enjoyable life) versus the expenditure on those items.

Then, the stress ecology process examines and evaluates the relationship of the items in your stress environment. It is much more than simply moving sticky notes around. Through the strategies in Chapter 5, beginning on page 51, you'll reorder your stress environment to support your capacity for a purposeful and enjoyable life by:

1. Eliminating items in your environment that detract from your capacity for a purposeful and enjoyable life
2. Identifying your "bubble" (the people in your life who need to be safe for you to be content)

3. Identifying items in your environment that are necessary to support your bubble

4. Examining the relationship of the items in your stress environment

5. Paying attention to intangible and ancillary benefits of the necessary items

6. Elevating the importance of items that enhance your vitality

7. Focusing on the items you identify as necessary and enhancing and letting unavoidable stress swirl on the outside

Section 3 details why security is the antidote to uncertainty.

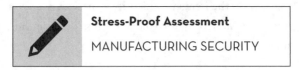 Problem #3	Stress-Proof Skill
Uncertainty crowds out rational thought.	Combat uncertainty by manufacturing security.

Stress-Proof Assessment

MANUFACTURING SECURITY

Uncertainty breeds stress and crowds out the ability to think critically and creatively.

Chapter 6, beginning on page 69, explores why your brain likes predictability and how you can train your brain to treat uncertain conditions as predictable.

It's not often that we spend a great deal of time contemplating the "what ifs" of life, but thinking through and preparing for unpredictable challenges increases your ability to deal with them efficiently and productively. It can also lower your stress level now and during a crisis. Security is an illusion because it doesn't prevent something bad from happening. We can manufacture the feeling of security in order to reduce stress, think critically and creatively, and enjoy life.

The exercise in Chapter 7, beginning on page 79, leads you through a process to thoroughly explore the source of uncertainty, the outcomes, what is necessary to control the outcome, and the behaviors required to practice responding rationally rather than emotionally. Over the years, I've helped people work through a variety of issues using this tool.

Manufactured security is a process, not a silver bullet.

Knowing what you need to have, know, and practice to move forward is essential, but you may need reminders and strategies along the way. Chapter 8, beginning on page 91, provides five additional strategies for cultivating a sense of real security and generating lasting stress reduction:

1. Notice and accept that fuzzy thoughts and mental paralysis are natural reactions to uncertainty.
2. Create a reminder of the work you've done to prepare.
3. Disconnect from the source of uncertainty to reset and refocus.
4. Behave your way to success.
5. Create artifacts of growth to fight mid-career malaise.

Section 4 offers a systematic way to offset the physical damage caused by high stress.

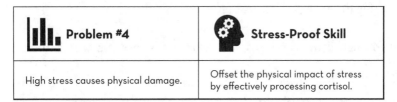

 Problem #4	Stress-Proof Skill
High stress causes physical damage.	Offset the physical impact of stress by effectively processing cortisol.

Stress-Proof Assessment

HOW MUCH DAMAGE IS YOUR STRESS CAUSING?
Find out beginning on page 107.

High cortisol levels eat away at physical health. Cortisol is the chemical your body releases when it senses stress. It is a natural, hardwired response. Prolonged stress, however, doesn't allow your cortisol level to return to normal and can damage your health.

Processing cortisol out of your body is essential to feeling better and protecting your health. Luckily, your body is naturally equipped to release cortisol, if you let it. Stress is a major risk factor for heart disease, and high levels of stress exponentially increase your risk of heart disease. This is why I call stress the Powerball of risk factors.

Chapter 11, beginning on page 127, provides eight strategies to help your body efficiently eliminate the stress hormone cortisol:

1. Raise your heart rate.
2. Change your breath.
3. Drink enough water.

4. Keep your body fueled.
5. Change your view.
6. Improve your sleep habits.
7. Don't give up.
8. Recognize the signs of trouble.

Section 5 identifies activities most likely to help you decrease psychological stress.

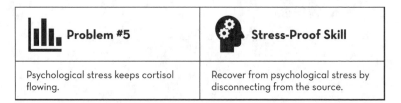

Problem #5	Stress-Proof Skill
Psychological stress keeps cortisol flowing.	Recover from psychological stress by disconnecting from the source.

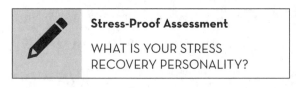

Stress-Proof Assessment

WHAT IS YOUR STRESS RECOVERY PERSONALITY?

Unlike physical stress, psychological stress often continues well after the stressful incident has passed.

Chapter 12, beginning on page 165, explores how to disconnect from the cause of stress, and recovery is an essential piece of stress-proofing. When we continue to think about a stressful situation or stay "revved up" about something, our cortisol level remains elevated. One of the frustrating symptoms of high cortisol levels caused by psychological stress is difficulty sleeping.

Shutting down the flow of cortisol allows your body to recover from stress. We all have different needs for distraction, contemplation, engagement, social interaction, and solitude when it comes to stress recovery. Understanding your personal needs is essential to choosing the activities most likely to allow you to disconnect and recover.

Practicing stress recovery goes beyond recognizing what works best to disconnect from stress. It requires recognizing the signs of high stress, being proactive in stress recovery, and actually doing something to allow for recovery.

Chapter 14, beginning on page 187, provides six strategies for psychological stress recovery:

1. Recognize the physical, behavioral, emotional, and cognitive signs that you need to recover from stress.
2. Be wary of contagious stress.
3. Be proactive rather than reactive in stress recovery.
4. Sip media, don't gulp.
5. Celebrate all victories.
6. Know when enough is enough.

Section 6 reveals why highly capable people are often unequipped to weather the stress of an unsolvable situation.

▮▮▮ Problem #6	⚙ Stress-Proof Skill
Vulnerability impedes resilience in crisis and change.	Get comfortable with vulnerability to become resilient in crisis and change.

Feeling vulnerable creates a stress reaction.

Life-threatening or life-altering events such as divorce, serious illness, and accidents leave us feeling helpless, unsafe, and weak—vulnerable. When we feel vulnerable, our natural inclination is to pull into ourselves for protection. Vulnerability makes it more challenging to engage in the world around us, connect with people who can help us, and feel good.

Chapter 15, beginning on page 203, explores why high-performing people are often inexperienced in accepting help and being vulnerable. For them, the stress of dealing with vulnerability amplifies the stress of crisis and change.

In the face of crisis and change, capable people fly into action and solve problems. When the problem isn't solvable or when we have to surrender to the idea of being helpless to change it, change and crisis hit highly capable people the hardest.

Chapter 16, beginning on page 209, offers eight lessons to get comfortable with feeling vulnerable for the times when all of the other strategies in this book are not quite enough:

1. Get comfortable with anger.
2. Accept help.
3. Give yourself a break.
4. Focus on what is possible rather than dwelling on what is difficult.
5. Notice the good stuff.
6. Embrace a sense of humor.
7. Let go.
8. Don't go it alone.

Conclusion: Practicing a Stress-Proof Lifestyle

Putting stress-proofing skills into action.

Stress isn't good or bad; it is a natural reaction to your environment. The skills in this book provide a system to deal strategically with the cortisol reaction so that you can live and work well under pressure, protect your health and emotional well-being, and enjoy life.

One of the ways I serve my audiences and readers best is to illustrate the connection between the information about their health (what we need to do) and the motivation for protecting it (why we do it). We all have moments in life we don't want to miss. For me, there are many: crying a little when we leave our daughters at college, seeing them fall in love, dancing with my wonderful husband at their weddings, and welcoming their children into our family. As a heart attack survivor, I can't rely on luck; I have to do the work to get there. We all do. I'm proud to provide the tools and motivation so that my readers and audiences get to have all their moments too.

The following process in the conclusion of the book, starting on page 231, walks you through how to create a plan to implement the stress-proof skills. I've spent nearly two decades asking people to change their behavior, and I have a few tricks to do it:

1. Don't try to change everything right now.
2. Create a small, specific, and achievable daily habit.
3. Connect what you want with what you need to do.
4. Reward yourself.
5. Don't get caught up in perfection.

> **"Life is not about perfection. It's about moving in the right direction."**

We all take a step off the path every once in a while. The key to making a change is getting back on the path.

Now that you've read the Executive Summary, I hope you flip through and find what you need to help you along your own path. You may also find the Leadership Insights in the next section helpful.

I wish you a lifetime of low stress and great success!

STRESS-PROOF LEADERSHIP INSIGHTS

Stress-proof leaders protect themselves from stress while propelling their people to do their best work.

Stress comes with the territory in most workplaces.

Too much stress impedes productivity, profitability, and wellness. The Centers for Disease Control and Prevention considers workplace stress the greatest occupational concern of the 21st century. Job stress is also a drain on companies' bottom lines, costing $300 billion a year through absenteeism, reduced productivity levels, and employee turnover, according to the American Psychological Association.

Where's Your Proof?
Check out more information about should read these studies starting on page 302.

I often call stress the "new smoking" based on studies by Stanford and Harvard Universities. In the United States, 25 million leaders rely on the productivity and creativity of the people they manage for their own achievement, and 28 million small business owners don't sleep at night because they're worrying about keeping their employees happy and the doors open.

Working with a wide range of organizations such as NASA, Colgate-Palmolive Company, Sprinklr, and Graef, I have been able to see what works to propel high-performing teams in the face of pressure and what doesn't.

Understanding how stress is triggered is the key to managing a worksite that is diverse in age, gender, ethnicity, and sexuality. Use the stress-proof skills for yourself and the following stress-proof leadership insights to manage your team.

High-achieving teams who can work under pressure provide their leaders with a competitive edge. Insights in this section equip managers and owners to use the solutions in this book to lead stress-proof teams and organizations, where members are productive and immune to the impact of negative stress. The nine Stress-Proof Insights for the Workplace include:

1. Self-sacrifice won't improve your team's performance.
2. Effective leaders solve problems so their people can work at their highest potential.
3. People perform best when they feel connected to their leaders, each other, and the mission of the organization.
4. Well-intentioned policies can undermine the value of work.
5. There are generational differences in how people react to uncertainty.
6. Other stressors impact reactions to overwhelm.
7. Effective leaders have courageous small conversations.
8. Resilient leaders are more successful.

9. Leaders typically believe they know what is causing stress in their team and commit time and money to addressing those issues. They are often wrong.

Insight #1: Self-sacrifice won't improve your team's performance.

Where's Your Proof?
Check out more information about my study on job stress on page 295.

One of the most concerning things I discovered in my research for this book was how many managers, executives, and business owners sacrifice their time, energy, and health in well-intentioned efforts to insulate critical employees from an overwhelming workload and protect the work-life balance of their people. Generational differences, change, and overwhelm can make the stress caused by the instinct to self-sacrifice worse. For example:

Gil is one of the last employees who worked closely with the son and grandson of the founder of the regional garden center business. With more than 30 years in the business, Gil still holds to the traditional values of the company, including working until the job is done, no matter how long it takes, especially during the very busy spring planting season. His company makes most of their money in the six weeks between Memorial Day and July 4th.

As a buyer, Gil manages a team of younger workers and finds their lack of work ethic frustrating. He, however, needs to retain the employees he trains and often finds himself working extra hours so that his team members can have "work-life balance." His long hours, however, are taking a toll on his health and his relationships at home. He feels squeezed between the needs of his staff and the need to get the job done. He also chafes against the executive team hired by the family who still owns the company but is no longer involved in the day-to-day operation. The executives came from business or marketing backgrounds and don't have the same love for the garden business. Gil is frustrated by the revolving door in the executive suite, feeling the company he loves is just a stepping-stone to the next job for most of the executives.

Ironically, Gil's instinct to take on more to protect his people not only increases his stress, it also signals a lack of trust in his employees, which contributes to their uncertainty and stress. Organizational culture expert Lisa Haen agrees: "When a leader takes on the team's work, it devalues the team. Team members are left to wonder about their role on the team and their ability to succeed in the organization."

Who's Who in the Book?
Learn more about Lisa Haen on page 308.

The habits and work style of the leader influence the stress level and productivity of the team. If a leader works long into the evening, team members feel insecure leaving earlier. If the boss never takes vacation, workers feel uncertain about taking their vacation time. If a leader "protects" the team from decisions made by upper management and does not share how hard he or she fought for the team's view, the team doesn't have all of the information necessary to trust the leader's commitment.

If you want to change the performance of the team, think about whether what you do supports what you want to see. "To change the behavior of the employee, we often have to start by looking at the behavior of the leader," says Lisa.

Please stop sacrificing yourself for "the good of the team." It doesn't work. Implement the stress-proof skills in this book to protect yourself from stress instead.

- Be honest—are you sacrificing yourself?
- How is your sacrifice impacting your performance and your health?
- How is your sacrifice impacting your people?

Insight #2: Effective leaders solve problems so their people can work at their highest potential.

People don't leave jobs; they leave work environments. Work culture was the third highest cause of stress in my research. Interestingly, while only about 20 percent of people said work culture caused their stress, more than 30 percent said an improvement in work culture would reduce stress.

Over and over in my work, I have seen organizations weather significant overwhelm and uncertainty while maintaining high job satisfaction. Employers who root out problems and make their people feel seen, valued, and connected to the mission of the organization endure change and high stress and support employee retention and engagement.

Bill Sennholz, president and CEO of Forward Bank, put it this way: "Every employee is a brand ambassador. We can't have them financially stressed or wondering if they'll have a job next year. We have to be the employer of choice in our region to be the bank of choice."

Who's Who in the Book?
Learn more about Bill Sennholz and Forward Bank on page 310.

In a tight labor market, competing for the best talent is a top priority. Not only does Forward Bank actively listen to their employees to define the problems to be solved, they also proactively communicate about the direction of the organization. In addition, they have an internal marketing budget dedicated to educating their employees on the benefits of working for the bank as compared to other regional employers. Employee satisfaction is the goal.

Forward Bank demonstrates dedication to employee satisfaction in small actions, such as buying dinner for employees who work late to complete a project, and big actions, such as creating the Pay It Forward Fund, which provides grants to employees in financial crisis. I saw all of this in action when I presented at their annual all-staff "Epic" day. They were celebrating being named one of the "Best Banks to Work For" by American Banker. What made the award so much sweeter was that the survey from American Banker was completed by all of the employees on the system changeover day, which was the culmination of a two-year, all-encompassing, stress-inducing, massive conversion of the bank's operating system. Despite moving to a new building, overhauling the operating system, and acquiring other banks in that two-year period, the employees reported 95 percent job satisfaction. CEO Bill Sennholz attributes this level of satisfaction to the commitment of the organization to make decisions based on whether they serve the success of their two stakeholders: depositors and employees.

Clearly, the employees feel connected to that mission!

"Our Forward Family working together is the only way we reach our goals, and one of our goals is to be the best—the employer of choice in our area. We have reached that goal again, repeating on the list of Best Banks to Work For 2018 by American Banker. Even more exciting is the announcement that Forward received a Bubbler Award: Best Places to Work for Young Professionals in Wisconsin."

Ultimately, leaders can solve problems and intentionally increase the value of work, reduce stress for their people, and improve performance.

- What problems do you need to solve for your people? (If you don't know which problems to solve, please see Insight #8.)
- What are the intangible benefits of working with you?
- How do you communicate the value of those benefits to your people?

Insight #3: People perform best when they feel connected to their leaders, each other, and the mission of the organization.

As we discussed in Section 2, we can change the value of an item in our stress environment by focusing on the intangible benefits. How we are allowed to work, when we work, how we are evaluated, and whether we like the people around us are all part of what makes up the value of work. Your people have to see more than just the numbers on a check.

Figuring out how to create value is the key.

As companies struggle to retain millennials and create more productive teams, many workforces have become less physically connected, and it is harder for employees to feel connected to each other, their leaders, and the organizational purpose. The draw of a remote workforce is alluring. Not only does it decrease brick and mortar costs, but the theory is also that remote employees enjoy better work-life balance, less stress, and are likely to stay with the company longer.

But is this true? Not really.

While work-life balance issues aren't the top stressor for any of the employee groups in my research study (remote, traditional, men, women, parents, etc.), more remote employees reported work-life balance issues than those who work in conventional offices with the same company. Even more worrying, the remote employees reported higher overall stress levels as well.

Why are remote employees more stressed?

Three issues appeared over and over in the comments on my research survey:

- **Remote employees feel disconnected from their peers and the mission of the organization.** Even the name "remote employee" suggests a distance between the employee and the rest of the team. Missing out on day-to-day conversations and in-person meetings can result in a remote employee being steps behind in a fast-moving project. Other comments suggest that being isolated from the camaraderie built by working in the same physical space makes remote employees feel like the outsider who can never fully join the team. Finally, remote employees often aren't aware of how their contributions are connected to the overall success or mission of the organization. Employees need to feel valued, and that is hard to achieve for those who are physically disconnected. Remote employees are more likely to look for other work.

- **There is no line between work and home when your office is there.** Working from home or the local coffee shop may sound great, but the reality is that for everyone—whether in a traditional or home office—work and life happen simultaneously. Going to the office does provide some natural division of what is "work" time and what isn't. Without that division, it can be hard to block out the call of personal issues to get work done, and it can be equally difficult to draw a line where work time ends.

- **Scheduling demands can be challenging for remote employees.** One of the more common comments from remote employees in my research is the challenge of working in different time zones. Other people said that they wished they could work on their own schedule rather than having to log in during traditional work hours.

- **All of this became more relevant as people were forced to work remotely because of COVID-19.**

So, is working remotely always more stressful? Not necessarily.

One of the companies I worked with, Titus Talent Strategies, has a 100 percent remote workforce. In preparation for their annual meeting, their employees used my anonymous job stress testing instrument to diagnose what was causing stress in their organization. Notably, none of their employees reported issues with work-life balance.

How do you connect remote employees with each other and the organization's mission?

It starts with language. One of the first things Titus Talent Strategies CEO Jonathan Reynolds shared with me was that Titus Talent is a MOBILE workforce, not a remote workforce. His understanding of making employees feel valued goes well beyond semantics, however.

Who's Who in the Book?
Learn more about Jonathan Reynolds and Titus Talent Strategies on page 311.

Team and organizational communication is a top priority, and they continually articulate and support their shared mission. Titus Talent has a set of what they call "lived values" that govern how they work together and with clients.

Employees are empowered to work according to their own rhythms. For example, night owls aren't forced to be productive in the morning. Titus Talent measures success based on work product rather than hours logged.

During my program at the annual meeting, I had the pleasure of leading a discussion about the culture of the organization. Many expressed the feeling of being a part of a physical team despite working in different parts of the country. It was clear they all felt the benefit of working for a company that is genuinely invested in employees as individuals.

Titus Talent is a great example of implementing policies to create connections that increase the intangible benefits of work.

- How do you connect with your people?
- How do your people connect with each other?
- How do you connect people with the mission of the organization?

Insight #4: Well-intentioned policies can undermine the value of work.

People like to be told they are doing a good job.

Policies to encourage employee retention can backfire if they are not aligned with the mission and ultimate success of the organization. If I could wave a magic wand and make one change to reduce stress in corporate America, I would get rid of the practice of giving everyone an evaluation of "meets expectations" except for one person who is awarded "exceeds expectations." Why should a single team member receive an "exceeds expectations" evaluation?

An expert on potential, Thom Singer, says, "Systems are important, but if they limit people from innovation and trying new things, the company and the individual cannot grow and expand." This type of policy increases stress and decreases performance in a few ways. For example:

Who's Who in the Book?
Learn more about Thom Singer on page 309.

First, it increases stress for the leader.

Jennifer, a senior manager in her 50s, is squeezed between corporate policies and managing her team effectively, especially when dealing with the two managers directly under her. Louis has been with the company for more than a decade and Cole is a new millennial hire. They both work hard and are valuable members of the team. She is allowed to give only one employee the review rating of "exceeds expectations" necessary for promotion. Jennifer is required to have a plan to promote millennial employees every 9 to 18 months. She had two millennial employees leave within a year of being hired, and her boss has made it clear that she needs to keep Cole in the company. Both Cole and Louis do a great job, and Jennifer doesn't want to choose between them. She feels that she has to award Cole the "exceeds expectations" evaluation but dreads the conversations ahead.

Second, the practice devalues work and feeds career malaise.

As we discussed in Chapter 8, people need to feel like they are growing and succeeding. When Louis asked Jennifer what he could do to exceed expectations next time, she didn't have any answers. The evaluation doesn't reflect his performance, and there is nothing he can do to change it in the future. Jennifer tried to explain that Louis's raise and merit pay package were not dependent on the rating, but it didn't matter to Louis. He feels invisible and isn't likely to take on anything extra. He also feels like he's been pitted against Cole and only one of them can succeed in the company.

Finally, arbitrary policies sow uncertainty and mistrust in the organization.

Trust in the leadership of the organization is an essential factor for success. If people distrust their leaders, they are more likely to leave. My study revealed that uncertainty and distrust destroy employee retention and engagement.

How do you create policies that increase the value of work?

Be predictable.

"Organizations want to be agile, to react to market changes quickly, but change for change's sake just increases uncertainty and stress unnecessarily," says Lisa Haen, an expert on agile organizational culture. We discussed in Section 3 that stress caused by uncertainty impedes the ability to perform. Making the outcome of an uncertain situation predictable decreases stress and increases performance. Agility requires the same type of predictability. "People need predictable responses and support in order to perform. Constant change by nature is unpredictable and reduces organizational agility," says Lisa.

Get buy-in from all angles.

People support what they help to create. "If you haven't included representatives of each group impacted by the policy, you've already failed," Lisa adds. For example, input from each stakeholder group in the annual review process—executives, upper management, middle management, and employees—not only would result in better policies, but also in policies supported at all levels.

This is also important when designing employee benefit, rewards, and wellness programs. These are intended to elicit specific behaviors that will either increase productivity or decrease costs, such as medical insurance expenses. Ultimately, organizations want to support actions that increase the company's bottom line. So why do so many employee reward programs fall flat? Too often they fail due to lack of buy-in at one or more levels: individual, top-down, and lateral.

Encourage individual buy-in.

Individual employee buy-in hinges on making sure employees understand the "what's in it for me?" aspect of the program. For example, yearly biometric screening (i.e., rating an employee's blood pressure, blood sugar, body mass index, and cholesterol against a desired standard and rewarding them for meeting that standard) can feel intrusive and dehumanizing. Treating all employees the same, whether they have healthy habits or not, makes people feel invisible. Failing to reward progress toward healthier results is disheartening. If an employee loses weight and improves their biometrics, shouldn't that be celebrated, even if they don't yet meet the desired standard?

Framing the behaviors in terms of the benefit it provides to the individual and rewarding the behavior in a way that matters to that individual increases the chances of compliance.

For example, the same biometric testing can be used to keep track of the impact of stress and help employees recognize the importance of healthy habits for reducing this impact. As we discussed in Section 4, stress can increase blood pressure and other heart disease risk factors. Recognizing an uptick in biometric readings can alert people to the need to make changes to limit the impact of stress. We've established that we need to be able to offset the stress of the job to do the job well. Framing exercise, eating well, and other healthy behaviors as a way to offset stress can be very effective in engaging employees in a wellness initiative. For example, using the results of an annual biometric screening in conjunction with this book gives employees a framework to choose healthy behaviors that will ultimately support productivity as well as limit health care and absenteeism costs.

Employee rewards work only if people want them.

Just like a gift, a reward can be interpreted as worthless, thoughtless, or worse—insulting or a burden. Consider the gift of a puppy. If you wanted a puppy, it is a great gift. If you are a cat person, the gift of a dog is thoughtless. If you look at the puppy and see a poop machine ready to chew up your favorite shoes, the gift is a burden.

Do your employees value the rewards you offer?

Asking employees what they want is a critical component of great employee rewards. Many of the things employees want don't cost much to provide. For example, most people would open-field tackle their best friend for an extra day off or to be able to leave at 3:00 P.M. on Friday. Some of the leaders with whom I talked pushed back on the idea of using time off as a reward based on the reduction of productivity. But think about what we all do when we know we are going to be away from work: we make sure to tie up loose ends, scramble to get things finished so we don't have to think about them, and hustle to clear our inboxes. In other words, people tend to be highly productive in advance of time away from work. What would motivate your employees?

One more thought...

Don't call them employee rewards if they aren't.

Psychologically, rewards are positive reinforcement. The reward entices the behavior and makes it more likely that the behavior will be repeated. It's the "carrot." Removing a punishment is not a carrot. For example, some companies increase the cost of employee health coverage and then require health-related behaviors to reduce the cost. The increased cost is negative reinforcement, a "stick," used to motivate behavior. To avoid the penalty, people must participate in biometric screening, health coaching, etc. Avoiding being hit by a stick isn't a reward. Calling the discount of health care contribution a reward is confusing and destroys trust.

Purpose-driven companies carefully develop employee reward programs to support behaviors that improve employee experience, productivity, and the bottom line.

Top-down buy-in:

One of the most popular strategies to reduce occupational stress is to "leave work at work." It is a wonderful strategy in theory. Workers are encouraged to disengage from work activities at the end of the workday and not re-engage until the following workday. The rule that no one should send work e-mails between 7:00 P.M. and 7:00 A.M. doesn't work if your boss regularly sends e-mails at 11:00 P.M. If we see that e-mail, our brains automatically start tackling it. It isn't a choice; we are wired to address the issue at hand. The Midwest Region of the American Heart Association has the best example of how to foster a culture of "leaving work at work." The staff is regularly under enormous pressure to raise funds, support research, and educate medical professionals and the public. The pace can be grueling, and the association knows it must protect their people from high stress and burnout to maintain the best talent. Sure, some people may choose to work long hours during crunch time, but they use technology to delay e-mails until the morning. In addition, they close their offices between Christmas and New Year and during the week of July 4th. During those weeks, the top-down directive is that no work should be done. The common e-mail responder explains that all e-mail will be answered when the break is over. None of this is possible without buy-in from the C-suite on down.

Lateral buy-in:

For a policy or program to work, it has to work for all of the teams, departments, or factions in an organization. Policies that make sense in an office may cause issues on the manufacturing floor. Leaders from across the organization must support the policies and programs and have input in creating them. If one department is burdened unfairly by a policy or informally opts out when a leader doesn't support or enforce it, the policy cannot be effective.

Ultimately, organizational policies either align with the culture of the organization or become the culture of the organization.

If your policies, benefits, or rewards make your people feel invisible or disenfranchised, that is the culture of your organization. As we discussed in Insight #3, people perform best when they feel seen, valued, and connected to the mission of the organization.

- Are your personnel policies aligned with the mission of the organization?
- How do you tell your people they are doing a good job?
- Is your evaluation process fair and an accurate reflection of performance?
- How do you involve stakeholders in policy development?
- Do your rewards and benefits make your people feel valued and seen?
- Do your employees value the rewards and benefits you offer?
- How are you generating individual, top-down, and lateral buy-in?

Insight #5: There are generational differences in how people react to uncertainty.

Sorting the data from my study by age and gender revealed new insights into the problems and solutions of intergenerational work relationships. For example, teams made up of millennials and led by boomers or Gen Xers tend to have an unhealthy dynamic that I have confirmed in hundreds of interviews. Unlike their boomer and Gen X counterparts, millennials are not interested in playing the long game at work. It all comes down to the expectation of trust. Leaders have to understand this dynamic to manage a productive workforce.

This dynamic comes into sharp focus when there is uncertainty in the organization. Whether the uncertainty is caused by layoffs or poor communication about the direction of the company, the generations react differently.

- **Boomers** came of age in a time where hard work and long hours paid off with raises and promotions years down the road. They generally trust that their organization will have their backs in difficult times. However, boomers fear that their career will end before they are ready to stop working, and this fear can be paralyzing because they don't see any other option.

- **Gen Xers** tend to hunker down and work defensively in uncertainty. The prospect of looking for another job seems scarier than staying put. They entered the workforce trusting their leaders but have learned to be suspicious. The stress of staying in an uncertain environment decreases their creativity and productivity. This defensive posture at work makes them less likely to take on new projects, offer critical insights, or take any kind of risk. Uncertainty, in effect, guts the potential of these workers, which could have a considerable impact on the bottom line.

- **Millennials**, however, are warier and more protective of their efforts than the other two generations. People in this generation have told me time and again how they saw their parents come home carrying the contents of their desk in a cardboard box. They learned early on about the emotional devastation of losing not only a job but the loyalty and protection of a trusted employer. They have also noticed that the traditional incentives for staying with a company, such as a pension plan, have been removed. Millennials have good reason to believe that long-term payoffs aren't in store for them, so the cost of performing high-pressure work for the implied benefit of delayed gratification isn't worth it for them.

At the first whiff of uncertainty, millennials start looking at their options. Again, they do not have faith that the organization values them, and they are not going to be the last ones out the door. If things are going downhill, they choose to get off at the top rather than waiting for the crash. As one employee of an enterprise-based social media management company put it, "I'm not sure I can wait around to see how this works out. I have loans to pay off."

How will the next generation of workers react to uncertainty?

Time will tell, but having raised two young women of that generation, I have some thoughts. This group grew up with an entire world of information at their fingertips, and they've been trained to sift through it and evaluate its trustworthiness. This may be the most information-literate generation we have ever had. As they enter the workforce, they will fact-check and source-check information with remarkable speed and acuity. They are looking for proof that the organization can be trusted by vetting every communication. This means employers who try to "spin" bad news with corporate double-speak will be seen as untrustworthy sources of information.

Employee retention is predicated on trust in the organization. If leaders want people to stay with the organization during change, market uncertainty, growth, and challenge, they will have to communicate messages of security and trust tailored for each generational audience.

- Are you communicating the security of the organization in ways that promote trust?
- How are you addressing different generational needs for trust?

Insight #6: Other stressors impact reactions to overwhelm.

We all bring different life experiences to the table. A variety of viewpoints produces the best creative results, but it also generates differences in how we react. When a new project is presented, some on the team may be elated with the opportunity while others groan at the idea of taking on yet another thing. Same project—different reactions. Work doesn't happen in a vacuum. Leaders need to consider the influences that may impact the reaction to overwhelm, such as:

- A project that involves travel out of town may be exciting to some, but for a single parent or someone caring for a loved one who is ill, it presents significant challenges.
- Presenting at a large conference may be a great opportunity, but not for someone who has maxed out their credit card and can't book the airline ticket, even if it is going to be reimbursed.
- People who have to talk differently or hide parts of their personal lives at work so they will be accepted are already highly stressed. Anything that creates a feeling of vulnerability will intensify stress.
- High-performing people don't usually say "no" when asked to take on something new. They will endeavor to rise to

the challenge, regardless of the impact on their stress, wellness, or overall performance.

We can't always know what others experience, but we can be genuinely curious when people react in a way we didn't expect. Asking nonjudgmental questions and listening with sincere interest are the keys to leading well.

- What life experiences of your people are different from your own?
- What questions do you need to ask before you make assignments?

Insight #7: Effective leaders have courageous small conversations.

Leaders know that addressing changes in behavior at work, such as suddenly coming in late, missing deadlines, or appearing depressed or apathetic, is essential, but they are often reticent to begin a conversation that may uncover a deeper issue. Leaders need to be courageous and forge ahead in small conversations despite the discomfort. "The best gift to a team is for a leader to be there," says Chip Lutz, a retired Navy officer who has spent the last decade training leaders, working with the military, and helping service people before and after deployment. "Talk to your people and find out what is happening."

Who's Who in the Book?
Learn more about Chip Lutz on page 311.

Most of us are uncomfortable starting a conversation about mental health, addiction, suicide, or even the death of a loved one or the end of a relationship. We don't know what to say or what to offer. Offering help is a more comfortable type of conversation for both parties. An employee assistance program (EAP), for example, is often the best-kept secret in a company. Through an EAP, companies provide services at no cost that can be incredibly helpful, but most people don't know they are available or won't remember in the moment. For example, EAPs can help employees:

- talk with an attorney about an estate, divorce, adoption, or child custody
- receive financial counseling
- get help with relationship issues (at home and at work)
- find grief support
- talk with someone about drug addiction (their own or family members')
- speak with a counselor about mental health issues (family members are usually covered as well)

Connecting a distressed team member with resources to address their problem may eliminate one of the biggest hurdles to access—the embarrassment of asking for help. This is a reason for leaders to follow up proactively. Creating a calendar appointment to reach back out to an employee who shared a severe diagnosis of a spouse with you, for example, is not only compassionate, it protects the performance of that employee. Many caregivers try to do it all and don't know how or when to ask for help. Checking back in provides the opportunity to offer support through the EAP and discuss whether using Family Medical Leave Act benefits might be appropriate. Too often an employee's performance degrades to the point of discipline or firing when they could have taken a leave if it was offered.

You don't have to stage an intervention; rather, start with a small conversation. "People are uncomfortable with the topic of mental health and don't know how to have a conversation about it," says Chip. His advice is, "If you see something, say something. Ask about what is happening." If their answers are concerning, ask, "Are you thinking about harming yourself?" Chip notes that many people worry that talking about suicide will push the person toward an act of self-harm. "Don't worry about that," he advises. "We all go through bad times, and people don't know where to turn. It's not a time to mind your own business. Ask the question." He suggests the next question is even more important: "Do you have a plan?" Take the answer seriously.

Chip suggests that everyone keep the National Suicide Prevention Lifeline number (800-273-8255) in their phone. You can also text HOME to 741-741. I put together a list of mental health resources, which you can find at StressProofResources.com.

Small conversations matter. People who feel seen and valued perform better and stay longer.

- What resources are available to your people? (Your HR team can be your best resource.)
- What changes are you seeing in your people?
- What small conversations do you need to start?

Insight #8: Resilient leaders are more successful.

"As a leader, you have to develop strong resilience muscles. You have to know what grounds you and refuse to veer away from it. Risks are necessary, and failure is often inevitable. You can't give up," says Grace Colón, PhD. Grace is the CEO and president of InCarda Therapeutics, a clinical-stage drug delivery company pioneering a novel approach of treating acute cardiovascular conditions with inhaled medications. Developing new medications and bringing them to market is a high-stakes game that requires raising millions of dollars, all on the promise of better treatment. She knows the importance of resilience.

Who's Who in the Book?
Learn more about Grace Colón, PhD and InCarda Therapeutics on page 312.

Grace credits resilience for her success raising $50 million so far to develop an inhaled treatment for acute paroxysmal atrial fibrillation (afib) events within minutes. "Everything we do is focused on the people who need a way to treat afib as quickly as possible without a visit to the emergency room." When challenges arise, Grace refocuses her team, board, and investors on the people who need a solution. "It comes down to planning for challenges and believing in the purpose of the organization. It's the underlying resilience muscles that make the difference."

Grace contends that this is why companies led by nontraditional (women and minority) founders and CEOs are more likely to have a better return on investment. "Nontraditional leaders have to be more resilient and creative with fewer resources. They succeed because they have to work harder." For example, it can take nontraditional leaders three times longer to raise the same amount of money as white male leaders. Grace indicates that this is because the discussion in the room is different. For white male leaders, investors discuss the size of the opportunity. For a nontraditional leader, the discussion focuses on the risks of the investment. "When you live every day with a thousand little insults," she says, "you learn how to plow through and move forward."

As we discussed in Section 6, resilience is a choice, but it is also learned behavior. I like Grace's idea of resilience muscles. Every mistake, failure, or challenge provides an opportunity to build the skills to move forward in the face of more significant problems. Caregiving, parenting, and social challenges all build skills to deal with higher-level issues. In my research, the organizations that were clear on their purpose and that empowered their people to see risks and failures as part of the process were the most successful in weathering challenges.

- What life and work experiences have strengthened your resilience muscles?
- How clear is your commitment to the purpose of your work?
- How are you empowering resilience in your people?

Insight #9: Leaders typically believe they know what is causing stress in their team and commit time and money to addressing those issues. They are often wrong.

Organizations are surprised when my testing instrument reveals the truth. Digging into a vast array of businesses to understand what actually causes stress has been fascinating. As an outsider with an anonymous tool to collect data, I get the unvarnished truth and deep insight from employees into what is creating stress in the organization. This information is the key to choosing the right solutions.

I can always tell if a team is in trouble by the length of answers to the open-ended questions in the instrument. As part of my research, I package a stress reduction program for the employees with the testing tool and report to management to deepen insight into the team. Observing office interactions and interviewing employees and leaders is enlightening.

For example, I worked with a company with a "Glassdoor problem." Glassdoor is like Yelp for employers, and the mostly millennial employees of the organization expressed their dissatisfaction on the popular website, citing work-life balance issues. My Stress-Proof Testing Tool, however, revealed a different story, one not solved by the organization's open-concept offices, flexible work hours, and ample snacks.

The employees worried about the speed of change in the company, the future, and the possibility of losing their jobs. Also, the rapid growth and international nature of the business created an overly complex technical system, causing employees to log into more than five separate systems to complete their work. Poor communication about changes and lack of transparent leadership were top stressors.

On the day of my presentation, I saw this in action when the new leader of the international sales division arrived at the branch office with no notice. As he met individually with some team members in a glass-walled conference room, palpable tension rose in the rest of the office. Rather than alleviating concerns, the well-intentioned but unexpected visit fed employees' stress.

Change is a catalyst for stress.

As we talked in the office, the employees made their discomfort clear. They craved less uncertainty and more security.

Why didn't the organization's leadership see the need to address change and stability?

According to a report by the National Institute for Occupational Safety and Health, evaluation of occupational stress levels and causes are subjective and can be skewed by internalized bias as well as managerial and organizational priorities. An unbiased third party is more likely to identify the sources of stress in the organization and the organizational, managerial, and individual strategies best suited for addressing them. To uncover the causes of stress in your team or organization, visit StressProofYourTeam.com and request a link to my Stress-Proof Testing Tool. Groups of 20 or fewer members can access the tool for free.

The frank feedback from the Stress-Proof Testing Tool exposes managerial blind spots as well as easy opportunities for improvement. This information is key to choosing the right solutions and avoiding making the situation worse.

My client's problem couldn't be solved with a work-life balance solution because work-life balance wasn't the problem. Once they knew that uncertainty about rapid growth and change as well as complex technology were the issues, it was possible to identify the real solutions to those problems.

Even the most well-intentioned stress reduction initiative can backfire if the actual cause of stress isn't uncovered.

Anita, the manager of a business office of a major university going through budget issues that were resulting in layoffs, contacted me about a stress-management program. The well-intentioned wellness committee decided to offer yoga at lunch to calm the waters and improve morale in the support staff, but the problem was getting worse. Some of her team members weren't talking to others, and the tension in the office was palpable. Surprisingly, the testing instrument revealed yoga at lunch was causing significant stress within the team.

- First, some of the employees were angry about money being spent on a frivolous class instead of increasing their salary.

- Others were upset that their concerns about workload and time off were going unheard, and they felt they were being treated like children.

- The few employees who did participate in the program reported it reduced their stress temporarily; however, the employees who had to stay behind to answer the phones were not happy and considered the employees taking yoga as "not doing their fair share."

In the testing tool, employees indicated three things would reduce their stress:

- First, they desired more effective communication with leadership.

- Second, they wished leadership would either hire more staff or make an adjustment to the expectation of productivity with a smaller team.

- Third, they needed more efficient systems. The employees were using out-of-date software that didn't allow data to be transferred into reports quickly.

I was able to reveal these issues to Anita in a report with recommendations to reduce stress and improve productivity. She wasn't able to change the software or hire more staff immediately, but she was able to have candid conversations with her team. By acknowledging the challenges of the software and staffing levels, she validated the team's concerns.

Through some creative scheduling, Anita was able to continue to provide yoga for those who enjoyed it, permit some quiet time in the office for those who needed that, and allow two employees to come in early and leave early a few days per week. She is working to make room in the budget to update the software. Overall, morale is better.

With careful analysis of the causes of stress revealed by the testing instrument, leaders can proactively manage team environments to increase performance.

Communication is often the key to addressing the cause of stress in the workplace. For example, when I worked with an association of health care information managers, their employees' most significant stressor was the field's extremely high expectation for productivity and accuracy. At the time I worked with them, new government regulations required a change in the way health care service billing was coded, which resulted in companies having to update or completely overhaul their software systems. The workers were not only learning new codes but also navigating new systems. Their learning curves were steep. One employee described it like this:

"It's like learning a foreign language while using a software program designed to make your job more difficult, and all the while your supervisor is breathing down your neck about meeting goals."

They worried that their jobs were in jeopardy because they were necessarily less productive and making more mistakes as they learned. Some were looking for new jobs to escape their stress.

These results shocked the managers I interviewed. They felt confident their team knew the new demands would be taken into account when review time came around. Too often, I see managers who feel sure they've communicated their message, but their employees either haven't heard it or haven't heard it enough to believe it. Emphasizing the end goal front of mind and celebrating small steps toward it keep the lines of communication open and let people see progress.

- Are you solving the right problems?
- What will you do to uncover the cause of stress in your team?

ABOUT ELIZ GREENE

Eliz Greene is ridiculously excited about stress.

She not only finds the chemical reaction in the body caused by stress fascinating, but stress is also her favorite topic to speak about, write about, and discuss in line at the grocery store.

With a surgically repaired heart, Eliz also knows stress management isn't a "nice-to-have," but rather an essential survival skill. Surviving a heart attack at age 35 while 7 months pregnant with twins propelled Eliz on a mission to share her story to inspire other busy people to pay attention to their health.

Just days after her heart stopped and she endured open-heart surgery and a cesarean delivery, Eliz held both her daughters together for the first time. Amazingly, despite the pain and uncertainty, what she felt most strongly was contentment. Her priorities were crystal clear. She knew she'd been given a second chance at life and a unique perspective for a reason.

For nearly two decades Eliz Greene has traveled the country sharing her story and down-to-earth, well-researched methods to improve heart health. She honed practical and implementable strategies to manage stress for herself and the thousands of audience members and readers she reaches each year.

Her research uncovered the secrets of how purpose-driven organizations create corporate cultures that are immune to overwhelm and uncertainty.

As a keynote speaker and worksite wellness consultant, she has worked with organizations such as NASA, Colgate-Palmolive Company, Kowa Pharmaceuticals America, United Parcel Service, Nationwide Mutual Insurance Company, Merck, Boston Scientific, WE Energies, IEWC Global Solutions, South Dakota Public Health Department, Society of Women Engineers, Association of Women Lawyers, and the American Heart Association. She was chosen to represent the future of the speaking industry by the National Speakers Association at its 40th anniversary and has presented numerous times on the business of speaking.

She's been profiled on CNN, PBS, Lifetime, TNT, and has been interviewed on countless national and local news programs.

Eliz is a seasoned spokesperson for campaigns such as the American Heart Association's Go Red For Women initiative and the Take Cholesterol to Heart campaign, a joint initiative of Regis Philbin, Howie Mandel, the American Academy of Family Physicians Foundation, and Kowa Pharmaceuticals America. Public relations and advertising agencies leverage her speaking platform and social media standing to advance their messages through traditional and earned media.

The American Heart Association presented Eliz with the Heart Hero Award in 2010 for her work in advocating for the HEART for Women Act, lobbying Congress, raising awareness, and educating health care professionals on the unique needs of women with heart disease.

Eliz is an author and writes a top health and wellness blog. She was named as a Top Online Influencer on stress and heart health. She has been recognized as a medically ethical blogger for providing well-researched and responsible information.

She holds a degree in communications from the University of Wisconsin–Madison with a focus on research. In order to provide scientifically relevant data on job stress, she worked with a professor emeritus from the University of Wisconsin–Madison to develop the research study.

Eliz is a leader in the speaker profession. She led the National Speakers Association's Academy for new speakers at both the national and chapter levels for more than a decade. She has been on several strategic task forces during times of transition and has led two dynamic diversity groups within the organization.

In addition to her degree in communications, Eliz is also trained as an adaptive movement specialist, dance teacher, and choreographer. She uses her adaptive training to create implementable strategies for health and stress management for people of all needs and challenges.

An avid sailor, Eliz enjoys time on Lake Michigan with her husband, Clay, and their beautiful (now adult) daughters.

CONNECT WITH ELIZ GREENE

High performance under pressure

Eliz brings groundbreaking research on job stress and leadership and *immediately implementable* solutions to help teams lead, perform, and feel better. Her high-content keynotes and trainings are wrapped in *humor, memorable stories, engaging activities,* and *motivation* to go back and do something different.

Stress-proof your leaders, your teams, and your heart!

Hire Eliz to speak at your event or train your leaders & employees:

Reach out to our team:

www.ElizGreene.com

Kate@ElizGreene.com

414-207-6878

Visit Eliz's blog:

www.EmbraceYourHeart.com

Join Eliz's page on Facebook:

www.facebook.com/elizgreenespeaker/

Connect with Eliz on LinkedIn:

www.linkedin.com/in/elizgreene/

Subscribe to Eliz's YouTube channel:

www.youtube.com/elizgreene/

Check out the latest Stress-Proof products, downloadable worksheets, and videos:

www.StressProof.Life

Share your Stress-Proof journey comments and intentions:

www.IWillBecause.com

WHERE'S YOUR PROOF?

With every word I write and speak, I strive to provide evidence-based and responsible information. Over the years, I've read more studies and articles than I can count on heart disease, nutrition, stress, workplace dynamics, and mental health. I've referenced several in this book. The citations for and (sometimes tongue-in-cheek) summaries of those studies follow the synopsis of my own study on job stress below.

What causes stress at work?

Study author: Eliz Greene

Referenced on: pages 19 and 259

In November of 2015, I launched a research study focused on quantifying the causes of workplace stress. This was initially conducted to quantify the problem of work-life imbalance and create better stress management strategies.

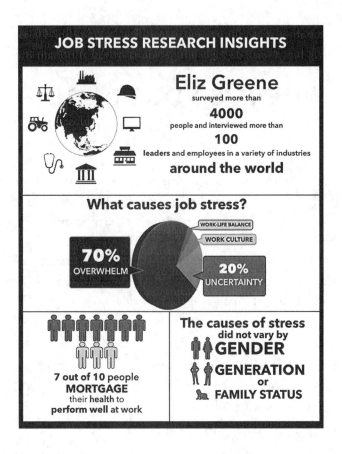

The results were shocking: 93 percent of all groups, including men, women, parents of young children, and millennials, reported that their stress cannot be relieved by common work-life balance strategies such as time management, mindfulness, or meditation. Also concerning was that 70 percent of participants indicated that they were stressed half of the time or more at work (a level high enough to cause physical damage) and that 30 percent reported that they were stressed most or all of the time.

More than 4,000 international survey responses and over 100 in-depth interviews with executives, managers, employees, and business owners revealed that the old methods of work-life balance solutions such as flexible hours, office space redesign, healthy living, exercise programs, mindfulness, and time management aren't working.

The real causes of job stress

A broad cross section of industries and job titles participating in the job stress study revealed interesting patterns about the underlying causes of job stress. Not surprisingly, staff reductions, budget constraints, and the national economy have resulted in challenging stress environments at work. In fact, 7 percent of people in the study indicated that their stress level was not going to get better because a high degree of stress was just part of the nature of their job.

To further analyze what causes job stress, the initial phase options were expanded to include the top three to four issues causing stress at work, not just the top factor. Only 4 percent of people indicated that work-life balance issues were a top concern; the rest stated that their stress was caused by uncertainty, a negative work culture, or overwhelm.

Stress Reduction By Category

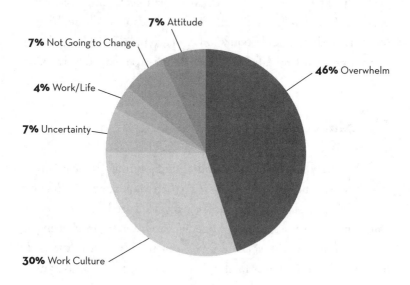

7% Attitude

7% Not Going to Change

4% Work/Life

7% Uncertainty

46% Overwhelm

30% Work Culture

Stress caused by uncertainty

One of the most common themes in the comments in the job stress study is concern about the instability of the national economy, government policies (particularly for respondents in health care fields), layoffs, market uncertainty, wage issues, and change. In our study, 18 percent of respondents indicated an uncertain future was their top source of job stress.

For example, responses from the higher education staff participating in the first phase of the study expressed deep worry about the trend of small or absent raises in light of budget constraints. While many value the school and their fellow employees, they wonder how long they can stay in a job with a downward income against the rising cost-of-living trend.

When asked what would reduce job stress, only 7 percent of respondents indicated something related to a more secure future would reduce risk. Those suggestions included:

- Job security
- Better compensation
- Better national economy
- Better regulations
- Better government
- Stable organizational structure

Many of the comments suggest that the respondents do not expect these conditions to change, but rather anticipate having to endure them over time. This likely explains why fewer people suggested a stress reduction factor related to an uncertain future would reduce job stress.

Stress caused by work culture

A negative work culture was a top stressor for 7 percent of study participants, but 30 percent indicated that a more positive work environment would reduce their stress.

Among the stresses reported were:

- Negative co-workers
- Poor relationships with a boss or supervisor
- Communication issues
- Lack of teamwork
- Weak organizational management
- Poor leadership

Suggestions for reducing environmental stress included:

- Better management
- Getting rid of problem employees
- Better communication
- More transparent leadership

When asked what employers had done to reduce stress, many responded that their boss was the primary cause of their job stress. Others indicated that administration did not take the issue of job stress seriously. A small percentage did, however, indicate that their boss did a good job of managing stress. Examples included allowing flexibility in schedule, approving sick time, defending the employees against demands of upper management, and building a good team.

Stress caused by overwhelm

Overwhelm was the top stressor for a vast majority of respondents. Three of the top five reported stressors were:

- Getting everything done in the time allowed
- The pace at work
- Missing something important

Altogether, 68 percent of people said some aspect of overwhelm caused stress, such as:

- Making a mistake because there is too much to do
- Demands of productivity
- Demands of accuracy
- Doing more with fewer staff

When asked about reducing stress, 45 percent of people also indicated that a change related to workload would help, including:

- Adjusting expectations of accuracy or production during times of low staffing or systems change
- Hiring more staff
- Implementing better training
- Improving systems or technology
- Reducing workload
- Getting rid of unimportant tasks
- Eliminating micromanaging
- Adding resources
- Not being expected to do work after hours
- Improving staff reliability

Many people again commented that these issues are unlikely to change due to budget constraints. Few people indicated their employer had done anything to address workload. Being trusted to complete work without interference was mentioned twice as positive aspects of management. Also, a few people offered praise for bosses who have realistic expectations of workload and help prioritize projects. A small percentage of people indicated that changing their own attitude about work or work habits would reduce stress.

In summary, overwhelm, work culture, and uncertainty are the primary causes of job stress. Some of these issues must be endured rather than resolved. Other factors, such as the quality of management, negative co-workers, and communication, are able to be addressed only at an organizational level. Addressing overwhelm is most likely to be successful in reducing job stress.

Computations of Uncertainty Mediate Acute Stress Responses in Humans

Study authors: Archy O. de Berker, Robb B. Rutledge, Christoph Mathys, Louise Marshall, Gemma F. Cross, Raymond J. Dolan, & Sven Bestmann

Published: *Nature Communications* 7, no. 10996 (2016): 1–11, https://doi.org/10.1038/ncomms10996

Referenced on: pages 72 and 73

Quick summary: I found this study's use of small electric shocks to examine people's stress very interesting. When subjects knew they would either absolutely receive a shock or absolutely not receive a shock, they were less stressed than when receiving a shock was uncertain. I do wonder how they got people to agree to participate.

Workplace Stressors & Health Outcomes: Health Policy for the Workplace

Study authors: Joel Goh, Jeffrey Pfeffer, and Stefanos A. Zenios

Published: *Behavioral Science & Policy* 1, no. 1 (Spring 2015): 43–52, https://www.hbs.edu/faculty/Pages/item.aspx?num=50306

Referenced on: page 257

Quick summary: This study pulls together information from 228 other studies on workplace stressors and health outcomes, revealing that job insecurity, high job demands, and long work hours are detrimental to employee health.

Disparities in State-Specific Adult Fruit and Vegetable Consumption

Study authors: Seung Hee Lee-Kwan, Latetia V. Moore, Heidi M. Blanck, Diane M. Harris, and Deb Galuska

Published: *Morbidity and Mortality Monthly Report* 66, no. 45 (November 17, 2017):1241–47, http://dx.doi.org/10.15585/mmwr.mm6645a1

Referenced on: pages 147 and 148

Quick summary: Some very smart people say we should eat more produce.

Sleep Modulates Haematopoiesis and Protects against Atherosclerosis

Study authors: Cameron S. McAlpine et al.

Published: *Nature* 566 (2019): 383–87, https://doi.org/10.1038/s41586-019-0948-2

Referenced on: page 155

Quick summary: This study explores how sleeping too little increases your risk of heart disease.

Sleep Deprivation: Impact on Cognitive Performance

Study authors: Paula Alhola and Päivi Polo-Kantola

Published: *Neuropsychiatric Disease and Treatment* 3, no 5 (2007): 553–567,

https://www.ncbi.nlm.nih.gov/pmc/articles/PMC2656292/

Referenced on: pages 154 and 155

Quick summary: This study explores how a lack of sleep makes you stupid.

Policy Perspectives on Occupational Stress

Study authors: Louise C. O'Keefe, Kathleen C. Brown, and Becky J. Christian

Published: *AAOHN* 62, no. 10 (2014), https://doi.org/10.3928/21650799-20140813-02

Referenced on: page 257

Quick summary: This report says we should treat occupational stress as a workplace hazard.

STRESS...At Work: CDC NIOSH Report

Report working group: Steven Sauter; Lawrence Murphy; Michael Colligan; Naomi Swanson; Joseph Hurrell, Jr.; Frederick Scharf, Jr.; Raymond Sinclair Paula Grubb; Linda Goldenhar; Toni Alterman; Janet Johnston; Anne Hamilton; and Julie Tisdale

Published: DHHS Publication No. 99–101, Cincinnati, OH: CDC, 1999, https://www.cdc.gov/niosh/docs/99-101/

Referenced on: page 257

Quick summary: This publication treats job stress as a threat to the health of workers and highlights what causes that stress.

The Relationship Between Workplace Stressors and Mortality and Health Costs in the United States

Study authors: Joel Goh, Jeffrey Pfeffer, and Stefanos Zenios

Published: *Management Science* 62, no. 2 (March 13, 2016): 608–28, https://www.gsb.stanford.edu/faculty-research/publications/relationship-between-workplace-stressors-mortality-health-costs-united

Referenced on: page 257

Quick summary: The results of this study indicate that employers need to pay more attention to management practices to control workplace stress.

WHO'S WHO IN THIS BOOK

A note about the two types of people referenced in this book:

I f they have a first and last name, they are real people and they have a short bio on the following pages.

If they have only a first name, they represent themes I've discovered in my work (except, of course, my husband and my daughters, who are very real and share my last name). I have the privilege of hearing stories from audience members, study participants, people I interview, as well as through comments on my blog and social media. Common themes of the impact of stress emerged over time in these stories. These themes are represented by the characters with first names only. Any resemblance to actual persons, living or dead, or actual events is purely coincidental.

I am indebted to the leaders and experts who shared their perspective with me. They are listed in order of appearance in this book:

Michele Payn, CSP is known as one of the leading voices in connecting farm and food. She works to simplify safe food choices while understanding food bullying. An international award-winning author, she brings common sense to the overly emotional food conversation and gets perspective from the cows in her front yard. Michele is a mom who is tired of the guilt trips around food, so she wrote *Food Bullying: How to Avoiding Buying B.S.* Michele and Eliz cohost the *Food Bullying*

Podcast based on the book. Michele is a professional speaker who has helped thousands of people understand the real story behind food. Her work has appeared in *USA Today, Food Insight,* CNN, *Food & Nutrition* magazine, NPR, and many other media outlets. Armed with science, compelling stories, and a lifetime on the farm, Michele upends the way people think about food. She is also the author of *No More Food Fights!* and *Food Truths from Farm to Table,* an IPPY award winner in health, medicine, and nutrition.

- Learn more about Michele at www.CauseMatters.com.
- Find Michele & Eliz's podcast at www.FoodBullyingPodcast.com.

Lisa Haen is a business consultant who works with leaders to design and develop an aligned culture strategy that strengthens systems and human capital. Together they create calculated culture micro-shifts that transform the workforce and build a leading culture that thrives and drives superior performance. Lisa used her background in developing cultures to support safety, human relations, and compliance in municipalities, utilities, and corporations to develop a data-based assessment of organizational culture.

- Learn more about Lisa's work at https://cultureinsideout.com/.

Chris Clarke-Epstein, CSP had a saying: Only writing is writing. As I sit down and stare into the blank computer screen, I often hear Chris's phrase reminding me that getting ready to write isn't writing. Turning away from the computer, I pick up my pen and start the practice of writing. Without fail, I write. Whether the words ever make it into the world is not the point. The next words may—and so I write. Mothers are told it is their voices that live in their children's heads. I know this to be true. Imagine how impactful someone must be to live in the head of someone who isn't even related to them. Chris's voice lives in my head, reminding me that I have something the world needs to hear. Her voice chides me to do the work. Her voice will be with me always and I miss her dearly.

Thom Singer, CSP has authored 12 books on the power of business relationships, sales, networking, presentation skills, and entrepreneurship, and regularly speaks to corporate, law firm, and convention audiences. He sets the tone for better engagement at industry events as the opening keynote speaker or the master of ceremonies. As the host of the popular *Cool Things Entrepreneurs Do* podcast, Thom interviews business leaders, entrepreneurs, solopreneurs, and others who possess an extra dose of the entrepreneurial spirit. The information compiled from these compelling interviews is shared with his clients, as he challenges people to be more engaged and enthusiastic in all their actions. Thom lives by the motto "Try New Things." After being a couch potato for most of his life, Thom is now an avid runner and completed his first half-marathon. As a lifelong "city kid," he has recently discovered the joys of nature. And after a lifetime of admiring stand-up comedians, he recently started performing in open mic nights and comedy shows.

- Learn more about Thom at
  https://thomsinger.com/.
- Listen to his podcast at
  https://thomsinger.com/podcast/.

Joanne Cantor, PhD is professor emerita at the University of Wisconsin–Madison, where she taught for 26 years. Her focus is on the psychological impact of the media and technology on people's cognition and emotions. She is widely known for her research on children's fears from the mass media, the effects of media ratings and advisories, and media violence effects and interventions. She has won awards for her research, her speaking, and her mentoring of graduate students. She has published more than 90 articles in academic publications and has testified on numerous occasions before U.S. Congressional committees as well as the Federal Communications Commission. Her books include *"Mommy, I'm Scared": How TV and Movies Frighten Children and What We Can Do to Protect Them*, *Teddy's TV Troubles*, and most recently, *Conquer CyberOverload: Get More Done, Boost Your Creativity, and Reduce Stress*. She frequently talks about her research and gives advice for parents and the general public in national media outlets.

- Learn more about Joanne at http://yourmindonmedia.com/.

Bill Sennholz is the CEO of Forward Bank. Forward Bank was incorporated in Marshfield, Wisconsin, in 1919. Over the years it has grown to respond to changing needs. In the last 10 years they have moved into rural communities that larger banks were leaving and smaller banks couldn't sustain. Bill is also the president of the Marshfield Chamber of Commerce.

- Learn more at https://www.forward.bank.

Jonathan Reynolds is the CEO of Titus Talent Strategies, which created a model to make the recruitment and hiring process more efficient and effective. It's called Recruitment Partnership InSourcing (RPI). It's conflict free with the focus on becoming a team player rather than scrambling for an "easy fill." And bonus, this fresh approach can save you as much as 75 percent over traditional fee-based contingency recruiters. The organization exists to equip companies to make the best attraction, hiring, development, and engagement decisions to meet their company's people and performance objectives.

- Learn more at
  https://www.titustalent.com/.

Chip Lutz, Lt. Commander, USN (Ret), MS, MA, CSP, CHP is the president and founder of Unconventional Leader, LLC, and has 30 years of solid leadership experience. A retired Navy Officer, he has had two command tours and also served as the director of security for Naval District Washington, DC during September 11, 2001. In that capacity, he was responsible for the safety and security of 25,000 people on 6 different naval installations in the National Capital Region during one of our nation's most trying times. A seasoned educator and trainer, he is currently adjunct faculty for two different universities and has taught over 20 different classes in leadership, management, human resource development, and organizational behavior. Having spoken professionally full time since his retirement from the Navy, Chip has traveled all over the United States, sharing his message of leading unconventionally to organizations, associations, and military units.

- Learn more about Chip at
  http://www.unconventionalleader.com/.

Grace Colón, PhD is the president and CEO of InCarda Therapeutics. Dr. Colón brings over 25 years of experience in biopharma, genomics, health care, and industrial biotechnology. In addition to her role at InCarda, she is executive chairman (formerly CEO) of ProterixBio, and serves on the boards of CareDx (NASDAQ:CDNA) and on the advisory board of the Miller Center for Social Entrepreneurship at Santa Clara University. Formerly, she was a partner at New Science Ventures, a New York-based venture capital firm with over $700 million under management, and served on the boards of Paradigm Diagnostics, PerceptiMed, and Cocoon Biotech. Dr. Colón received her PhD in chemical engineering from the Massachusetts Institute of Technology, where she was an NSF Fellow. She also holds a BS degree in chemical engineering from the University of Pennsylvania, where she was a Benjamin Franklin Scholar. She was raised in San Juan, Puerto Rico, and lives with her husband and three teenagers in Los Gatos, California.

- Learn more about InCarda Therapeutics at https://incardatherapeutics.com/.

GRATITUDE

Most people breeze past the acknowledgment section of a book, so, first, I am grateful to you for taking the time to read it.

None of this is possible without the love and support of my husband, Clay. He is my biggest fan, my reality check, and the person most likely to make me snort with laughter. While most people give me credit—he is the organized, kind, funny, and reasonable one in the relationship! Thanks for putting up with me.

Our daughters continue to amaze me, and periodically drive me nuts—but that is the job of children, right? It is cool to be moving into the adult phase of our relationships, and I am excited to see what comes next. My proudest accomplishment will always be launching two kind, intelligent, and talented human beings into the world. I love you both.

We have wonderful family who has supported us along the way. I'm so grateful to my mom, Peggy Hughes; my sister and her husband, Meg and Brad Louwagie; and Clay's sister and her husband, Cyn and Mike McChesney. As I edited this book on lockdown during the COVID-19 crisis, I took laughter breaks with my sister and our cousins Adine Rodemeyer, Lanei Rodemeyer, and Robyn Hunt. Thanks for the giggles and support!

I owe a great deal to Kathryn Costello, my cousin and Excel expert. She took my data, did magic, and made all of the crunching work! Thanks, Kathryn.

If the key to success is surrounding yourself with people who inspire and push you...well, then my key to success has been joining the National Speakers Association. My fellow members have supported me—and kicked me into gear. On this project, I'm grateful to:

- Jess Pettitt, Thom Singer, and Gerry O'Brion, who are more than my mastermind group—they are my chosen family. Thanks for refusing to let me quit.

- Michele Payn, who asks hard questions. Thank you for inviting me to share your book journey and shepherding mine.

- Lisa Haen, who never lets me hide. Thank you for late-night conversation and day-time strategy.

- Chris Clarke-Epstein, who set the standard for being an author and speaker. Thank you for leading the way.

- Mellanie True Hills, who uses her story to change the world. Thank you for being my heart-sister.

- Sam Silverstein, who reached out to tell me it is time to step up. Thank you for introducing me to Sound Wisdom and for encouraging me.

- Mike Domitrz, one of my first mentors, who never let me settle for "just okay." Thanks for always telling me the truth.

I have some amazing friends who cheer me on. I am grateful to:

- Jill Holder Guy, my college roommate and everlasting friend. Thanks for always picking up right where we left off, no matter how long it has been.

- Angela Pierro, Ginny Gendelman, and Laura Kramer—thanks for turning serving on a school committee together into a friendship involving laughter, talking, and drinking a little wine (okay...not always a little).

- Our Friday night race crew: Jeff and Patty Greb, Jad Donaldson, Terry Schmidt, and Bob Heil. Thanks for coming out—we look forward to it every week.

- Mark and Cherie Stein—thanks for sharing the adventures of parenting and boat ownership with us!

www.soundwisdom.com